THE
Spoonflower
QUICK-SEW   PROJECT BOOK

THE Spoonflower

QUICK-SEW PROJECT BOOK

34 DIYs to Make the Most of Your Fabric Stash

ANDA CORRIE

Photography by Zoë Noble

ABRAMS | NEW YORK

CONTENTS

1

INTRODUCTION

About This Book

If you're like me, you have a stash of fabric that's been sitting in a room, just waiting for inspiration to strike.

While prints are fun to collect, it's *not* fun to see them gathering dust in the corner. Perhaps you found a great sale on fat quarters, or you inherited some fabric from your mother, or you have some leftover pieces from past projects and don't have the heart to throw them away. Why isn't there an easy way to find projects that are organized by the amount of fabric you have on hand?

This book is here to solve your dilemma. If you love fabric as much as I do, you'd appreciate some help bringing the textiles you have saved in a closet to life. It's time to unearth those treasured prints and make something that's purposeful and beautiful!

When we started Spoonflower in 2008, our mission was to empower creative individuals to design their own fabric and bring their beautiful visions to life. It was a novel idea at the time and quickly took off. Today, we have the world's largest marketplace of independent designs, and they are beloved by an audience of millions of customers. We're honored to be a starting point for so many crafters, quilters, makers, and small business owners. We love sharing our passion for DIY with a creative community worldwide—people like you.

Featured fabrics: Faces White by zoe_ingram, Constellations Light by holli_zollinger, Fishy by elliewhittaker

Whether this is the first time you've heard of Spoonflower or you've been a fan for years, it's amazing how energizing it is to connect with a company who values independent artistry and celebrates the pursuit of the creative spirit. In my own story, I started my career as a buyer for Saks Fifth Avenue, and after I got my MBA, I held various roles in marketing, advertising and product development. In 2013, after a few years of working at a national ad agency, I found myself wanting to return to my retail and consumer product roots, and began looking for a company to invest in that aligned with my passions and was a place where I could make a difference. Around that time, my sister was renovating her kitchen and wanted to get a roman shade made to go over her kitchen window. She found some fabric online and took it to a local sewist to have it made. The maker asked where she got the fabric, and when my sister replied that she found it online at Spoonflower, the maker said, "Ah! Did you know that they are local in Durham?" My sister was intrigued and reached out to Spoonflower to take a tour. When she shared this story with me, I thought, "How fascinating that a custom-printed textile company is in my own backyard." I reached out to the co-founders, Stephen Fraser and Gart Davis, to see how I could help this company grow. I was able to join the Spoonflower team in 2013, and now I help lead the company as co-owner and president (and one of its biggest fans).

In a magical moment of "worlds colliding," the creative possibilities with Spoonflower completely align with my own hobby and passion: interior design. If you visited my home today, you'd see Spoonflower designs on everything from kitchen tea towels, throw pillows, wallpaper, curtains, duvets, and art tables to dresses in my closet—I love infusing spaces with color and pattern, and my home feels like a personal reflection of my family and me. I believe *that* feeling of expressing yourself is what many of us are searching for with every stitch we make and every project we undertake.

A few years ago we came out with *The Spoonflower Handbook*, written by co-founder Stephen Fraser, Judi Ketteler, and Becka Rahn, which highlighted how to use our platform to create your own textiles and papers. In that book, we shared design-focused projects from how to make a pillow featuring your pet's photo to creating a handmade recipe tea towel—one of our most popular projects of all time. The content

Featured fabrics: Blackbirds on Peach by anda, Gold Paint Blobs on Cream by jenlats, Orbiting Celestial Bodies by friztin, By the Sea – Waves and Lighthouse – Cream by lemonni, Bebe Mudcloth by holli_zollinger

offers a great starting place for those wanting to get their feet wet with designing fabric, whether you dabble in watercolors or are a pro at Adobe Photoshop. (It even provides tips on how to sell your designs to shoppers!)

As we began dreaming up our next book, we asked ourselves: What would fabric enthusiasts need as a helpful resource? Every sewist has a fabric stash—some people have a shelf or even a room full. We decided that our focus would be on giving you inspiration to use those fabrics you might already have at home—or the ones you have your eye on, but haven't quite found a reason yet to add to your collection.

In fact, to make this book easier to use, we organized it by the amount of fabric each project needs, from swatches to fat quarters to yardage. Each DIY is endlessly customizable so you can make something that's entirely reflective of your style. Are you into watercolor florals or geometric animals? You can always head back to explore the Spoonflower Marketplace, where you'll find endless styles and artistic interpretations thanks to our international community of designers. You'll get to meet some of these amazing designers in the chapters of this book.

One talented designer we want to introduce you to right now is our friend Anda Corrie, author of this book. She has been a designer and handmade enthusiast with Spoonflower since the very beginning and is someone we often turn to for creative DIY projects for the Spoonflower blog. A former team member at Etsy, Anda is an illustrator, artist, mom and émigré living in Berlin, Germany. What we love about how she approached this book is that she doesn't neglect the small bits of fabric that we can't bear to throw away because they're gorgeous and still usable.

Go to your shelves now, and pick a fabric that inspires you. No matter what size it is, you've got what you need to get started with this book. Make the most out of what you have or get inspired by what could be—from little trinkets to future keepsakes you can enjoy for years to come. Whether you're trying out your first sewing project or are ready to devote a weekend to your dream DIY, we hope this handbook will be a go-to resource in your journey to handmade happiness.

Your fabric is waiting—let's get started!

Allison Sloan Polish

Allison Sloan Polish, President

Featured fabrics: Simple Palm Leaf Geometric by micklyn, Infinite Typewriter by mia_valdez, Zodiac La Luna Light by holli_zollinger, Watercolour – 16 by heytangerine, Fern on Green by littlearrowdesign, Monstera Leaves by crystal_walen, French Linen Tribal Ikat by holli_zollinger; wallpaper design Canal Gold Ivory by jenlats

The Basics

How to use this book

This is a book of sewing projects with instructions geared toward DIYers of all skill levels. Most require very basic sewing skills, so if you've threaded a machine before and understand how to sew lines and curves, you're going to do great! Or, if you've never sewn before, but are a quick study, you might pick up everything you need to know by following our instructions. Either way, we recommend consulting a sewing reference book or website and getting lots of practice if you really want to understand sewing.

We've arranged the projects in this book according to size, smallest to largest. If you're like us, you've got piles of unused stash fabric in all sizes in your craft room, and whatever their dimensions, there's a project in this book waiting to give them life. But, before we dive into projects, let's make some notions, trims, and tags for your completed handmade pieces. We'll even find a way to use those scrap bits from cutting, so you can *completely* empty your stash pile with zero leftovers.

What You'll Need: Basic Sewing Kit

This book is full of projects of all sizes that can be completed in an afternoon, provided you have all the materials. We recommend having the following supplies ready if you are working on a project that mentions the "basic sewing kit" in the Materials + Tools list for the project.

+ Sewing machine
+ Hand-sewing needles
+ Thread
+ Pins
+ Iron and ironing board

+ Scissors (fabric and craft)
+ Rotary cutter
+ Pinking shears
+ Paper

+ Dressmaker's pencils or chalk
+ Ruler and tape measure
+ Self-healing mat
+ Seam ripper

2

NOTIONS + TRIMS

A bit of trim, a little piping, or a lovely button can give you just the finish you need for the projects in this book.

At Spoonflower, we have found that making supplies from scratch can bring a lot of joy. Whether you're using fabric you've made with Spoonflower or using fabric from your stash, creating is all the more satisfying when each piece is unique. Plus, if you're a notions addict, you're going to love all of the options for embellishment these projects will afford you.

Learning to make your own notions and trims means you will always have what you need on hand when you start a project. So, why not set aside some time on a weekend to make making trims your goal? You'll never again be caught without that perfect finishing touch.

Featured fabric:
Crane Deco – Peach by lemonni

Bias Binding

Bias binding, we love you. Thank you for making seams so cute, edges easy to finish, and mistakes readily hidden. We use bias binding in many of the projects in this book, so let's sit down and make a pile of it.

First things first—when making homemade bias binding, your life will be *so* much easier if you spend a few dollars on a tool called a bias clip. It's a little metal contraption that looks something like this. They come in a few different sizes depending on the width of the resulting tape.

You can make bias tape with almost any amount of fabric. Did you know you can make a 29-inch (74 cm) strip of continuous 1-inch (2.5 cm) bias-cut fabric from one 8-inch (20 cm) Spoonflower swatch?

MATERIALS + TOOLS

Basic sewing kit (see page 12)
One square of fabric (8-inch
   [20 cm], 13-inch [33 cm],
   24-inch [61 cm], etc., as
   long as it is square)
Ruler
Washable fabric-marking pen
   (test on fabric first)
Bias tape maker
Rotary cutter
Iron

To make your own bias tape, you'll start with strips of fabric cut on the bias—a 45-degree angle to the fabric grain. Cut the strips to be twice the width of the bias binding you need. Although there are several ways to easily get a long, continuous strip of fabric, if you're making a ton at once or need a lot of bias tape for a project, this is our favorite method.

1 Begin with a square of fabric. Lay it flat on your work surface. With the fabric pen, draw a line diagonally between two corners and mark the top and bottom edges with a tiny A and the sides with a tiny B. Cut along the diagonal line.

2 With right sides of the fabric together, line up the two sides labeled A, leaving ⅜ inch (1 cm) of fabric extending past each end (photo A). Sew along that edge with a ¼-inch (6-mm) seam allowance, then lay the piece flat and press open the seam. Now you have a parallelogram.

3 Keep fabric right side down. Using a ruler and a washable pen, draw lines across the fabric **parallel** to the long side of your fabric parallelogram, at the width of the fabric strip you need (for example, draw the lines 2 inches [5 cm] apart if you are making 1-inch [2.5 cm] bias tape). If you have extra at the end, trim it to size.

The following fabric was used for this project: Spoonflower's Cotton Poplin in Flamingo Party (small) by shelbyallison

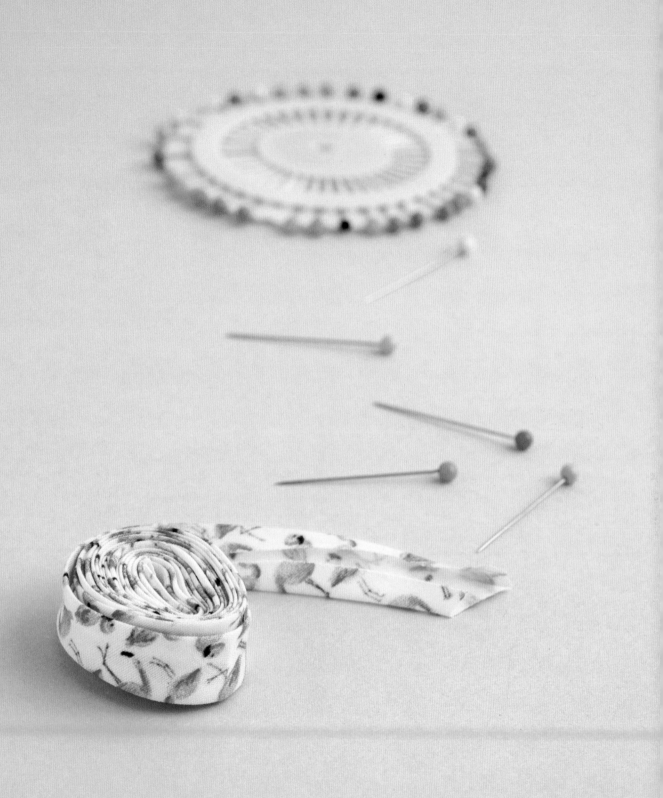

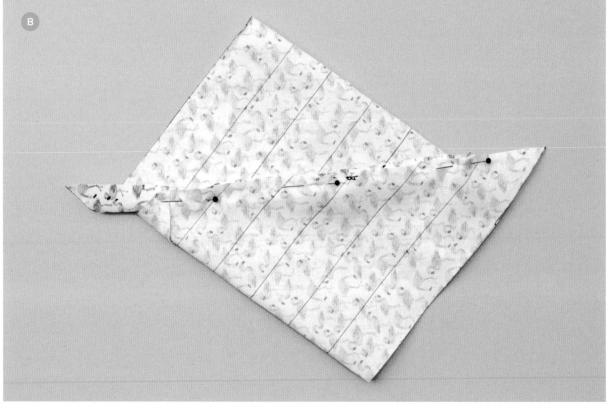

4   Line up the right sides of fabric labeled B as shown. The pencil lines won't line up, but will fall about ⅜ inch apart.

5   Sew a ¼-inch (6-mm) seam along this side (photo B). Now you'll have a sort of tube of fabric. Flip it right side out, and cut carefully following the lines you've drawn—resulting in one long, bias-cut strip of fabric (photo C).

6   Now, poke one end of the fabric strip into the wider end of the bias binding tool until it comes out the other side. It will come out folded. With the iron, press the fabric to fix the folds as you work the fabric through the tool.

Piping

Another trim you can make yourself with your long strip of bias tape is piping. Piping is used to add a coordinating or contrasting outline to projects and is great to have on hand to sew into the edge seams of pillows and cushions or even fancy beanbags (see page 39). Sometimes called cording or welting, it is quick work to make if you have a zipper foot for your machine and some cord (aka string in the thickness you want your piping to be). If you plan on using your piping in something you'll be tossing in the wash, always prewash the cord and fabric before cutting and sewing.

(see page 39)

MATERIALS + TOOLS

1-inch (2.5 cm) bias tape
  strip (see how to make a
  long continuous strip on
  page 16)
⁵⁄₃₂-inch (.4 mm)-thick cotton
  cording
Zipper foot
Basic sewing kit (see page 12)
Thread that matches your
  fabric

1   Follow steps 1 through 5 of making Bias Binding (page 16).

2   Place your cord in the center of the bias tape and fold the fabric strip in half.

3   Using a sewing machine fitted with a zipper foot, sew the fabric closed (about ½ inch [1.3 cm] when folded over), with the cord in the center. Use a long straight stitch, taking care to not sew through the piping cord.

The following fabric was used for
this project: Spoonflower's Cotton
Poplin in Yellow Buds Ditsy
by leanne

Covered Buttons

Matching buttons to fabric by using covered buttons—or deliberately *not* matching them—can give a project a wonderful charm. Commercial covered-button kits make these incredibly simple to whip up, but if you run out of shanks, you can make them just as easily without.

MATERIALS + TOOLS

Old buttons (flat or shank)
Fabric scraps
Thread
Leftover scraps of quilt
   batting (optional)

1   Start with a regular flat button, and cut a circle of fabric twice the diameter of the button.

2   Loosely hand stitch around the edge. Place the button in the center of the fabric disk and pull the thread tight to cover the button. Tie this off. Look, your button is covered—that's it!

3   You will still need to sew through this type of covered button in order to attach it to your project (you may need to guess where the holes are). Round shank buttons can be covered in the same way to get a more typical-looking covered button.

Tip:

+   If the button you're trying to cover has a lumpy surface, cut a tiny circle of quilt batting or fun foam the same size as your button and sandwich it under the fabric.

The following fabrics were used for this project: Spoonflower's Cotton Poplin in Bees at Work by ruth_robson, Cats Mint (small) by kimsa, and Daisies on Red by anda

Iron-On Patches

Spoonflower is full of designs with motifs in larger formats—perfect for transforming into decorative patches. When you're shopping or selecting a design online, note the size at which it's displayed (found underneath the fabric preview image). Make sure that the image is large enough for a patch. When designing your own patches, keep the edges simple—you'll be sewing around them later. A good general size for a single patch is between 1½ inches (4 cm) and 3 inches (7.5 cm). Leave a ½-inch (1.3 cm) space around the final design (choose basic repeat when uploading to Spoonflower). To make iron-on patches, we'll be using the magic of double-sided fusible interfacing, which is interfacing with a peel-off backing that adheres on both sides when pressed with an iron.

MATERIALS + TOOLS

Swatches of fabric with your patch motif

Thread in a coordinating color to your patch

Double-sided fusible interfacing as large as your patch

Basic sewing kit (see page 12)

1   To make a single patch, cut a piece of double-sided fusible interfacing that is about ½ inch (1.3 cm) larger than the image you're making a patch from.

2   Place it face down (backing-paper side up) on the wrong side of the fabric, on top of where the image is. Iron until adhered.

3   Cut out your design, leaving a ¼-inch (6 mm) border, and then sew around the perimeter of the design using a satin stitch, about ⅛ inch (3 mm) wide. Go slowly, and stop with the needle down to carefully lift the presser foot and rotate the fabric when necessary.

4   Trim off excess around the outside of stitching. Peel off the backing paper of the interfacing.

5   When ready to use, place the patch onto the desired surface, cover with light cotton cloth, and iron it on. (Before ironing, test the heat setting on a scrap of fabric.) You can reinforce the patch with stitching or simply leave as is.

The following fabric was used for this project: Spoonflower's Cotton Poplin in A Nod to the House Bird by katerhees

Handmade Tags

Tags can add a finishing touch to your handmade goods and are so simple to create with Spoonflower. For garments, try using cotton knit—it's soft, and there is no need to hem the edges of your tags. For bags, pillows, and other objects, my favorite tag fabric is silky faille or faux suede paired with fusible interfacing—like the patches we made on page 25, adding labels is as easy as ironing. Who wants to hem a million tags? If you do, try using cotton poplin and a rolled hem on your machine.

MATERIALS + TOOLS

Graphics software
One swatch of cotton knit or
  faux suede fabric of your
  tag design
Ruler
Rotary cutter
Double-sided fusible
  interfacing
Basic sewing kit (see page 12)

to design the handmade tags

1   Create a new file in your favorite graphics software that is 2 inch (5 cm) by 1 inch (2.5 cm) and 150 DPI.

2   Add guide lines (in Adobe Photoshop this is under View>New Guide) ⅛ inch (3 mm) around the entire rectangle. If your tag will be folded, add one vertically down the middle so you know where the fold will lie.

3   Design your tag within the guides. You could write your name or business, something adorable like "Handmade with love," garment care instructions, or put a drawing or logo on them.

4   Get fancy, if you like, with decorative borders and different colors. Once you are happy with the look of your tag, save and upload to Spoonflower, choosing basic repeat and ordering a test swatch of your design.

to make the handmade tags

1   For iron-on labels: Iron the double-sided fusible interfacing onto the back of your swatch. If making folded sew-in tags, skip this step.

2   Cut apart the tags with a ruler and rotary cutter.

3   Stack neatly in a spot in your crafting area where you will always have them on hand. When ready to use, either fold in half and sew into a seam, or peel off the interfacing backing paper and iron straight onto your project.

The following fabric was used for this project: Spoonflower's Organic Cotton Knit in Handmade Tags by anda

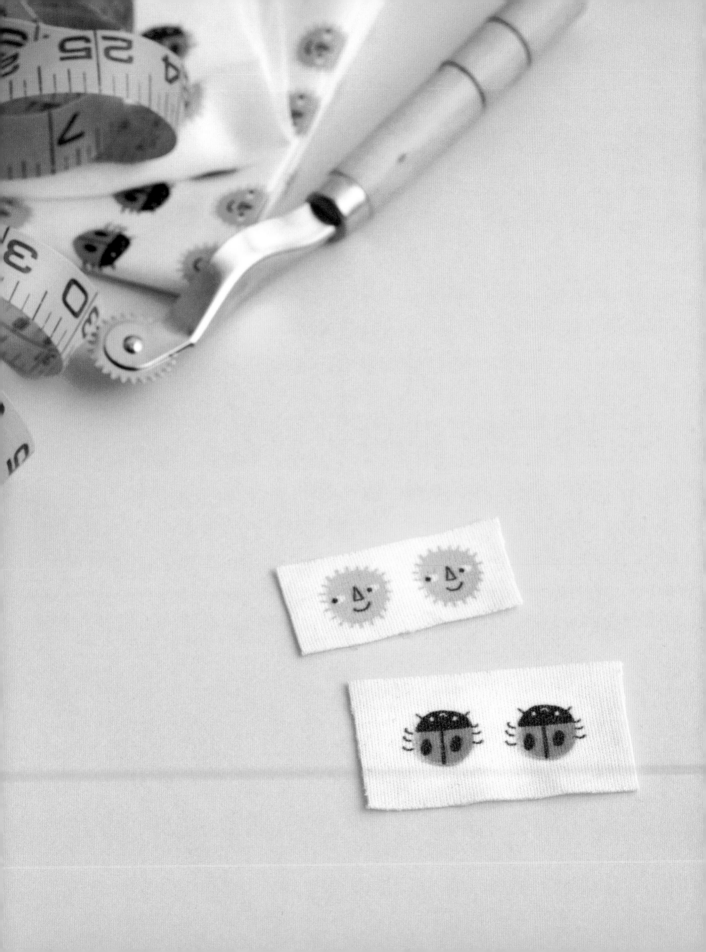

Jersey Fabric Yarn

Stretchy knit fabrics are perfect for making soft jersey yarn. You can make a big ball of this from a fat quarter of fabric and an *enormous* ball from a yard. Use it for tassels or braided headbands, crochet it into a rug, or macramé an enormous wall hanging.

1   Start with a rectangle of knit fabric with four-way stretch. (Spoonflower's Modern Jersey is perfect for this.) Trim off the selvage.

2   Now, starting at one corner, begin cutting a 1- to 1½-inch (2.5-4 cm) strip from the edge. When you reach 1 inch (2.5 cm) from the opposite end, turn the corner and keep cutting.

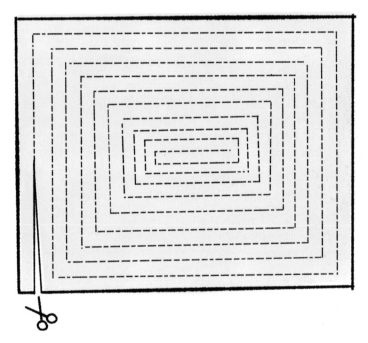

3   As you work, tug gently on the strip so the edges curl into themselves. You'll also probably want to ball up your yarn as you go to keep it nice and neat.

4   Keep cutting around and around your fabric until you spiral your way into the center and run out of fabric to cut. Voilà, jersey yarn!

The following fabric was used for
this project: Spoonflower's Modern
Jersey in City Life by friztin

Fabric Scrap Twine

Many of us are completely unable to throw away the scraps of any nice fabric and compulsively stash bits of it into bags until they are bursting at the seams. These pieces may be *perfect for a quilt*, we think. However, when you learn how to twist fabric into twine, it may change your life (and make your stash more manageable) since this is a project that will use all of your random fabric scraps. You can twist twine while sitting around watching TV, or while sitting in the sun for an afternoon drinking lemonade. Wherever you make them, the results will be beautiful! Here's the recipe.

MATERIALS + TOOLS

All your fabric scraps from similar fabrics saved in a big old basket, box, or bag
Scissors
Two hands & some patience

1 Cut or tear your scrap fabric into strips about 1 to 1½ inches (4 cm) wide, and as long as you like.

2 Grab two strips and hold them in your left hand. With your right hand, twist one strip in a direction **away** from your body. After two or three twists, bring the fabric strip **toward you, and over the second strip.**

3 Now take the second strip and twist the fabric away from your body. After two to three twists, bring it toward you and over the first strip.

4 Before you reach the end of a strip, grab a new strip of fabric and twist it along with the first one, thus working it into the twine (photo A).

Note: Try to use strips that are unequal lengths so they finish at different points in the twine.

5 Repeat until you have a mountain of fabric twine.

The following fabric was used for this project: Spoonflower's Cotton Poplin in Rolling Seas by ottomanbrim

Judy Quintero of shopcabin

Judy Quintero and her husband, Ralph, are the hard-working duo behind shopcabin, one of the top five design shops in the Spoonflower Marketplace.

Before shopcabin, Judy Quintero sold her designs on vintage plates through Etsy. As word got out and popularity grew, the couple expanded into home décor and began selling their designs on finished goods. Soon customers began to ask for coordinating prints in various fabrics.

Shopcabin designs are now featured on all sorts of handmade goods, and they have found a niche in the baby market, where their large-scale watercolor florals and other designs are perfect for wallpaper and nursery décor, and their smaller-scale animal and plant illustrations are ideal for baby bibs and rompers.

Pastels including blush, coral, and peach are strongly featured in her most successful collection. "I love colors and the power they have to inspire happiness," said Judy.

If you find a whimsical print from shopcabin that catches your eye, you'll likely receive a thank-you message from the shop owners themselves—no matter the size of your order. "Staying in touch with every one of our customers is the cornerstone of our success," said Judy.

The Fabrics

Take inspiration from the shopcabin line and don't be afraid to mix floral patterns with geometrics in your sewing projects. Geometric designs like Floral Dreams Quilt paired with florals (like Mini Floral Dreams) can complement each other beautifully, and create a fresh, modern look. Large-scale patterns like Floral Tropical Leaves work great on medium- to larger-sized projects like the knitting caddy or tent, while Patchwork Hens 5.25 is ideal for smaller ones, like the Two-Swatch Sunglasses Case (page 49) or the Travel Bag (page 86).

Three quick questions for Judy:

When did you fall in love with designing?

"When I was a little girl. I love colors and the power they have to inspire happiness."

What's in your toolbox?

"My Mac computer and a $100 fifteen-year-old sewing machine, which will probably be with me for life."

What's your mantra?

"I've got this!"

Featured shopcabin fabrics, from top to bottom: Mini Floral Dreams,
Western Flowers, Floral Dreams Quilt, Floral Tropical Leaves,
Barcelona Nights; border design Sweet Blush Roses

SWATCH PROJECTS

What can you make with an 8-inch square swatch? Quite a lot, it turns out, from herbal sachets (page 40) to toys (page 39) to adorable mini purses (page 42). Swatches are also perfect for projects that don't involve turning on your sewing machine at all— pretty little bits of fabric can decorate drink coasters (page 53), make gift-worthy pincushions (page 36), and more.

Our essential tools for experimenting with small projects are: hand sewing tools (because when working small, sometimes the machine actually makes things harder), fusible web (for attaching fabric onto any non-plastic porous surface), and stuffings of all varieties. Plus, many of the projects in this section can be expanded upon once you're comfortable. For instance, tiny beanbags are not that different from regulation corn hole bags (tip: Design the surface of your homemade corn hole board with Spoonflower's peel-and-stick wallpaper!). Or, while one mini banner makes a wall hanging, two dozen mini banners can make a garland. Once you have the basics down, the possibilities are endless!

We find that working small is inspiring and will put a dent in your swatch pile. Let's get started!

Featured fabrics: Sun Tile Sandstone
by holli_zollinger, Moonlight by lemonni

No-Sew Pincushions

After all the work you put into making notions in part two, here's a little break from effort. These no-sew pincushions are adorable and take just a few minutes to complete. The hardest part is finding the perfect containers to hold them—look for vintage teacups (toy sets are even better), espresso cups, tiny clay pots, or small ceramic planters at your local secondhand shop.

MATERIALS + TOOLS

Small container such as a toy
 teacup or planter
Swatch of fabric, almost any
 will work
Polyfill or cotton stuffing
Rubber band
Glue gun

1   Cut the swatch into a 6-inch (15 cm) circle. I usually trace around something round, like an embroidery hoop.

2   With fabric facing down, pile a big lump of stuffing in the center of it (photo A).

3   Gather the fabric around the stuffing. Holding it nearly closed with one hand, poke more stuffing into it until it's quite full. Seal with the rubber band (photo B).

4   Use a glue gun to attach the pincushion snugly into your container, rubber band side down. Glue the bottom first, then squeeze glue around the edges so it's neatly tucked into your cup or pot. Allow glue to dry for thirty minutes or according to package instructions and that's it! Add pins and it's ready to adorn your sewing table or be given to a lucky friend.

The following fabrics were used for this project: Spoonflower's Cotton Poplin in Rolling Seas and Book Fan by ottomanbrim

Basic Beanbags

Beanbags are a great first sewing project, particularly for children. In a nutshell, they are just two equally sized pieces of fabric and a bit of filling combined to make a toy! Once you can sew beanbags, you can use the same process to whip up herbal sachets for your closet, microwaveable eye masks filled with rice, and anything else in nearly any shape, following this format. Grab a few swatches from your scrap bag, and let's make some.

MATERIALS + TOOLS

One 8-inch (20 cm) swatch of fabric (almost any will do)

Basic sewing kit (see page 12)

Dried beans, rice, or feed corn (you can buy this in bulk if you plan on making lots of bags)

Herbal filling if making sachets (optional)

Length of piping if making fancy beanbags (optional)

1   Completing the following steps will allow you to create two beanbags from a single swatch. Using a ruler and pencil, measure, mark, and cut your swatch into four equal 4-inch (10 cm) squares.

2   Place two of the squares right sides together. Starting 1 inch (2.5 cm) from one corner, backstitch and then straight stitch toward the corner with a ⅜-inch (1 cm) seam. Work your way around the square, stopping 2 inches (5 cm) from where you began. Backstitch, and remove from the machine.

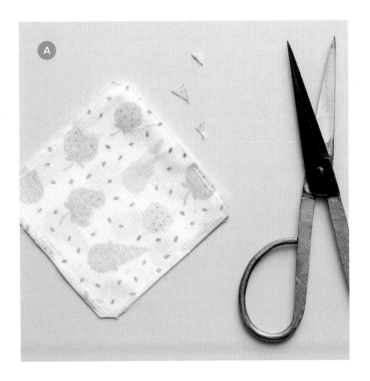

The following fabrics were used for this project: Spoonflower's Linen Cotton Canvas and Lightweight Cotton Twill in Blueberry by j_e_c_scott, and Back to School Pears and Strawberry Summer Party by heleen_vd_thillart

3 Trim the bulk from all four corners (photo A), and turn right side out. Using a funnel (or a bit of scrap paper rolled into a cone shape), pour your filling into the opening until the bag is about three-quarters full.

4 Topstitch with your machine or whipstitch by hand to close the bag.

Mini Sachets

1 Complete steps 1 through 4 as above, but make sure you use a natural, breathable fabric like cotton or linen. Replace the bean filling with your scented items.

Tip:

+ Need some inspiration for your sachet fillings? Try dried herbs such as lavender, mint, rosemary, and thyme, or dried flowers like gardenia, jasmine, lilac, peony, and rose. You can also use your favorite tea blends, cedar wood chips, coffee beans—any scent you love! Sprinkle essential oils into your mix to make it stronger, and add orris root to make it last longer.

Fancy Mini Beanbags

1   The steps above will get you a pretty basic beanbag. If you'd like a fancier version, just add some piping for an added touch.

2   Cut a 17-inch (43 cm) length of handmade piping in a contrasting or matching color (see page 21 for instructions on how to make your own piping).

3   Sandwich the piping between the two squares of fabric, beginning at one corner and leaving a ½-inch (1.3 cm) tail of piping extending outward. Line up the raw edges (photo A) and pin in place. At each turn, gently curve the piping to make rounded corners. When you reach the corner where you started, let the remaining piping extend past the hem, overlapping the beginning of the piping by just ¼ inch (6 mm) or so.

4   Sew around the fabric squares as above, but go slowly around each corner to avoid sewing through the piping cord. When clipping the corners, take care not to clip the piping—since piping is sewn on the bias, it will stretch and look fine when the project is turned.

Tip:
+   You can also leave your fancy mini beanbags unfilled to make cute drink coasters!

Tiny Circle Purse

This has to be one of the cutest things you can make from one swatch. This mini circle purse has a diameter of about 3½ inches (9 cm), large enough for most small treasures. Their size means they can be a bit finicky to make—some may have better luck with hand sewing instead of using a machine. We used a bias binding here to cover the inside seam and love how it looks (especially with mismatched and contrasting binding! It's like a surprise inside).

MATERIALS + TOOLS

One 8-inch (20 cm) swatch of fabric, any lightweight woven

10-inch (25 cm) purse zipper

A few inches of 1-inch (2.5 cm) wide bias binding in the same color of the zipper (see page 16 for instructions on making your own)

Two 3½-inch (9 cm) circles of fusible batting, interfacing, or craft foam to give the pouch structure

24 inches (61 cm) of ½-inch (1.3 cm) bias binding in any color and fabric (this goes in the inside and won't be seen unless the pouch is open)

Basic sewing kit (see page 12)

1   Cut out four 4-inch (10 cm) diameter circles from your swatch. (Four will fit side by side neatly in a 2x2 grid on an 8-inch [20 cm] swatch.)

2   Cut a 1½-inch (4 cm) piece of bias binding. Open the binding and place it right side down on the backside of one end of the zipper. Stitch ⅜ inch (1 cm) from the raw edges, being careful to hand crank over the teeth if necessary (this is less of a concern if you are using a plastic zipper). Flip the zipper around and repeat on the opposite end.

3   With the zipper right side out, fold it in half to line up the two ends of the opened bias binding. Stitch the binding ends together along its "double fold," or directly down the middle.

4   Refold the bias bindings around the zipper ends (in either direction) and topstitch each ¼ inch (6 mm) from the folded edge—it will be easier to do this if you open the zipper. See photo B for how this looks.

5   If you are using the batting/interfacing for structure, sandwich one of the batting circles between two of the fabric circles (right sides of the fabric out) and loosely baste with long stitches around the perimeter. Repeat with the remaining piece of batting and fabric circles (photo A).

6   Open the zipper—it will look like a number eight (photo B). Pin the perimeter of one basted fabric circle to the edge of the right side of one zipper half, and the second basted circle to the other half of the open zipper. You can tug the basting gently and slightly gather the fabric to make it fit exactly (photo C). Baste both circles to the zipper with your machine's zipper foot very near the edge.

The following fabrics were used for this project: Spoonflower's Cotton Poplin in Petites Etoiles by demigoutte and Watermelon Slices Coordinate by littlearrowdesign

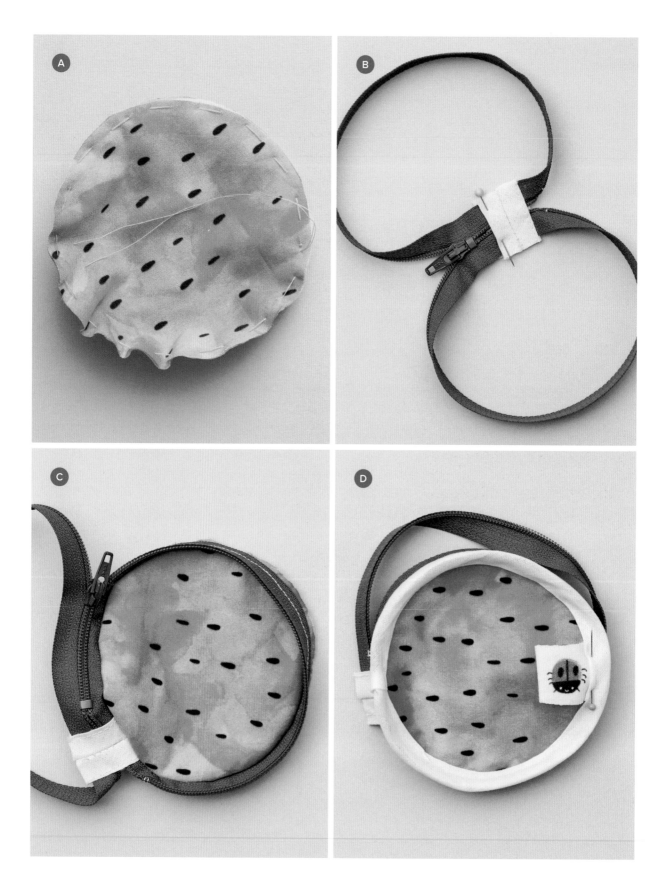

Note: Double-check that you are lining both to the right side of both zipper halves; when the zipper is open they look very similar! The "right" side is the side with the pull.

7   To finish, cover the inner seam with bias tape. Take your bias tape, unfold one side, and pin it right side down around the perimeter of the basted circle. This should overlap about ½ inch (1.3 cm) where you began.

8   Stitch a ⅜-inch (1 cm) seam using the zipper foot. Wrap the bias tape around and fold back under to cover the raw edges of the circle, then topstitch ⅜ inch (1 cm) around it. If you want to add a handmade tag (see page 26 for instructions), tuck it somewhere under the bias tape as you're topstitching (photo D).

9   Once you've gone all the way around and backstitched at the end, you'll have a neat circle of bias tape covering your inside seams. Repeat with the other half. Flip the pouch right side out, zip the zipper closed, and you're done.

Tip:

Different color zippers and fabric combinations make these almost mouthwatering:

+   Orange zipper + light orange or yellow fabric = orange slice
+   Green zipper + light green fabric = cucumber or lime
+   White zipper + brown fabric = sandwich cookie
+   Green zipper + red fabric = watermelon

Heleen van den Thillart of heleen_vd_thillart

Artist Heleen van den Thillart's work is a reflection of her desire to keep a childlike wonder about the world and stay true to what she loves. "Everything can be a tool," she says. "I use a variety of items when I am drawing, like crayons, chalk, acrylic paint, watercolors, pen and ink, and stamps."

After studying graphic design at the Royal Art Academy in The Hague she opened her shop, heleen_vd_thillart, on Spoonflower after entering a design challenge where she finished in ninth place. Encouraged, she added more designs, often channeling elements from the Netherlands or ideas for animals inspired by her kids.

The Fabrics

The classic color combination of blue and white works well on any number of projects. The smaller patterns on Tulips on Solid Blue and Pigeons in Royal Delft are best used for smaller projects like Fleece Mittens (page 79) or Basic Beanbags (page 39). The bolder, more scenic selections are great for covering more area. Be sure to line up the natural repeat in the pattern where possible to better orient the charming scenes.

Some great advice from Heleen:

What is your process when creating a new design?

"I can't just start sketching. I always start in my head first. So, I start with the internet and my bookcase for research. You can never have too many books. I can spend hours and hours in a bookstore, and I never leave empty-handed. Most of my books are about art or type design. When I start with a 'theme,' I look for what similar designs are already out there and think about what is still missing or how I can do it differently. I try to come up with at least 10 different design ideas. I like to put in some silly ones too. Never settle for the first thing that pops up in your mind. After a while, those silly ones might not be that silly after all."

The best advice I ever received is . . .

"Work hard and don't be afraid. 'Genius is one percent inspiration, 99 percent perspiration' is a quote by Thomas Edison. A teacher once told me that, and I totally agree! You can't just sit and wait for a brilliant idea to come. It won't happen. Just get going and don't be afraid to make a lot of mistakes. Making mistakes is a good way to learn. I try to teach this to my kids too."

Featured helen_vd_thillart fabrics, from top to bottom:
Dutch Square, Dutch Street, Pigeons, Holland, Bikes, Tulips;
border design Pigeons on Dark Blue

Two-Swatch Sunglasses Case

There is a lot you can make with an 8-inch (20 cm) square of fabric. This project takes two of them. When we're out of ideas but itching to sew, we always turn to zipper pouches. We love them for all the possibilities of fabric, shape, and construction—not to mention print/zipper/lining color combinations! For this project, we wanted something very straightforward, especially after the fussiness of the little circle pouches (page 42), and this project is perfect for giving your sunglasses a cheerful home.

MATERIALS + TOOLS

Basic sewing kit (see page 12)

Zipper foot

Two 8-inch (20 cm) swatches of silky faille or faux suede

Scraps of bias tape, about 3 inches (7.5 cm) (see page 16 for instructions on making your own)

One 6.5-inch (16.5 cm) closed-end zipper

7-inch (18 cm) square of 4-ounce quilt batting or 4 mm craft foam

Glue stick

The following fabrics were used for this project: Spoonflower's Faux Suede in Large Tropical and PomPom Fringe by jillbyers

1   Trim the selvage off the swatches until you have two 8-inch (20 cm) squares. Cut the lining fabric in half so you have two 4-inch (10 cm) by 8-inch (20 cm) rectangles.

2   We often cover the ends of zippers in tiny purses with bias binding so they look nice and neat without any effort later. To do this, cut your bias binding into two 1½-inch (4 cm) lengths. Unfold one side of the bias tape and align the unfolded edge with one end of the zipper (right side down, against wrong side of zipper). Stitch straight along the fold. You'll probably want to hand crank your machine past any teeth to avoid breaking a needle, although we're usually using nylon zippers and just zoom right over them capriciously.

3   Wrap the bias tape around the end to the front side of the zipper and, using your machine's zipper foot, topstitch the bias tape down (again, going slowly or hand cranking over the teeth). Repeat on the opposite end of the zipper to seal up the edges neatly.

4   Fold the outer fabric in half with right sides together and press. Unfold and place one side of the zipper face down against the right side of one long edge of the fabric. Place one half of the lining right side down on top so the zipper is sandwiched between the two fabrics, lining up all raw edges, and pin. Use a zipper foot to stitch ¼ inch (6 mm) from the edge (photo A).

5   Open it up so the zipper is poking out between the two pieces of fabric (now wrong sides together), and press (photo B). Refold the outer fabric and line up the opposite side of the zipper face down on the right side of the fabric, then pin the second lining piece with right side facing inward to the zipper and outer fabric—the side you've sewn in the last step

will also be between the two fabrics as shown (photo C). Sew a ¼ inch (6 mm) edge with a zipper foot.

6   Make sure all pieces are right sides together with the zipper attached in the middle. Open the zipper up, pin the lining sides together and the outer fabric sides together, and stitch a ⅜-inch (1 cm) seam along the sides.

7   Turn everything right side out through the zipper, so the outer fabric is on the outside, but leave the lining poking out of the zipper foot. Reach in with the glue stick and run it lightly over the wrong side of outer fabric— this bit of glue is going to help hold the batting in place. Take your 7-inch (18 cm) square of craft foam or batting, fold it in half, and tuck it into the pouch past the lining, pressing gently so it sticks to the glue (photo D).

8   With the lining still hanging out of the top through the zipper, sew the bottom of the lining closed with a straight stitch, trim the seam, and tuck the lining back into the pouch, enclosing the batting.

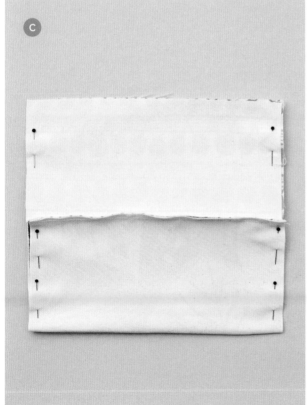

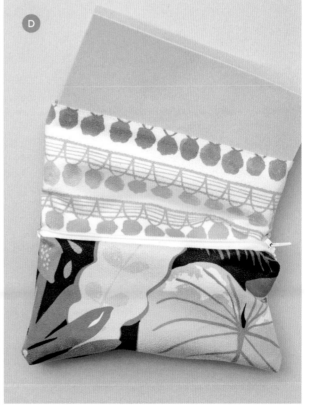

Drink Coasters

Summer fruits are a favorite motif for fabric, and a quick search of lemon, strawberry, or kiwi on Spoonflower proves there are loads of new ways to celebrate them. You can also use your favorite bright and colorful fabric from your own stash at home. These coasters are a super-fast, no-sew way to show off your favorite fruity and bright fabrics while protecting your furniture from sweating lemonades all year round.

MATERIALS + TOOLS

One 8-inch (20 cm) square
   swatch of silky faille fabric
Four 4-inch (10 cm) round or
   square cork coaster blanks
8-inch (20 cm) square of
   fusible interfacing
Ruler
Basic sewing kit (see page 12)
Mod Podge

1   If your fabric swatch comes with a white border, trim it off so that you have an 8-inch (20 cm) square of fabric.

2   Cut an 8-inch (20 cm) square of interfacing and line it up against the wrong side of your fabric swatch. Press with a hot iron until adhered.

3   Remove the backing paper of the interfacing and, using a rotary cutter and ruler, cut the swatch carefully into four 4-inch (10 cm) squares. Place each square of fabric right side up on a coaster, cover with a bit of cotton scrap fabric, and press for about 15 to 30 seconds until the fabric is adhered to the coaster.

4   If your coasters are round, trim edges off with scissors. Coat the surface with Mod Podge to waterproof your coasters.

The following fabric was used for
this project: Spoonflower's Silky
Faille in Lemons by stolenpencil

Mini Banner

Grandiose wall hangings and enormous framed prints are great, but what if you only have a teeny tiny space you're trying to decorate? These mini wall banners are quick to make and perfect for studios, craft spaces, lockers, and everywhere in between.

For our banner, we drew an abstract family portrait using basic shapes. First, we painted circles in various colors using paint markers to add simple details, keeping the finished design around 3 inches by 4 inches (7.5 cm by 10 cm). Next, we scanned our drawing, uploaded the image to Spoonflower, and ordered a test swatch on cotton sateen. Of course, you can also use a piece of fabric from your stash to make the banner and draw your design directly on the banner. Or use a favorite patterned print and leave it as is. There are so many possibilities for creating the perfect tiny banner.

MATERIALS + TOOLS

Scanner
White letter-sized paper
Pencils
Wide-tip paint marker
One 8-inch (20 cm) square
    swatch of cotton sateen
One 8-inch (20 cm) square of
    interfacing
7-inch (18 cm) length of a
    ¼-inch (6 mm) dowel
12 inches (30.5 cm) of baker's
    twine or embroidery floss
Basic sewing kit (see page 12)

The following fabric was used for this project: Spoonflower's Organic Cotton Sateen in a personal design by anda

1   Trim the selvage off your swatch so that it is an 8-inch (20 cm) square, then trim ¾ inch (2 cm) off each side of the swatch so that it is 6½ inches (16.5 cm) wide. Iron the interfacing onto the back of the square.

2   Measure 3¼ inches to the center of the bottom edge and mark (photo A). Measure 2 inches (5 cm) along the sides from each bottom corner and mark. Draw a line between the center mark and each side mark and trim off (your fabric will have a point).

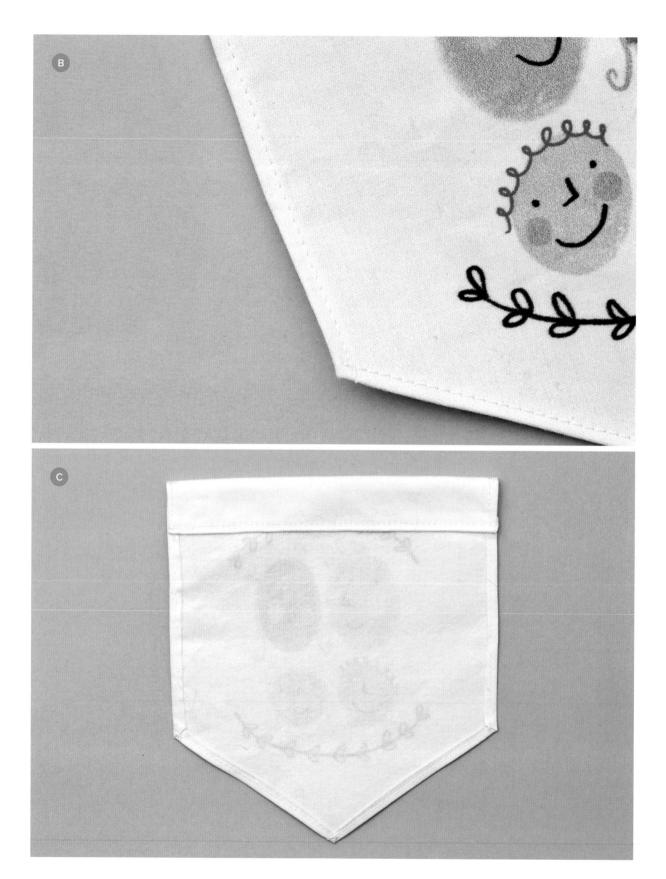

3   With the right side of fabric facing down, fold all raw edges over ¼ inch (6 mm) and press. Flip the fabric over and topstitch with a straight stitch around all sides, ⅛ inch (3 mm) from edge (photo B).

4   With the fabric facing down again, fold the top side over 1 inch (2.5 cm) and press. Flip, and topstitch ¾ inch (2 cm) from edge to create a casing (photo C).

5   Insert the dowel through this casing, tie baker's twine to each end, and hang.

Tips:

If you're uninterested in spotlighting your drawing skills (or lack thereof), then quotes, sayings, and inspirational messages make great banners, too. Type one out in a favorite typeface or write in your loveliest script. At a loss for words? Here are some ideas for generating banner messages:

+   Take a sheet of paper and a pencil and start jotting down any uplifting, inspirational word that comes to mind. If you find one you like but it feels too overused, look it up in a thesaurus for a fresh take.

+   What historical figures do you find inspirational or just simply fascinating? Search online for quotes under their name; chances are they've said something profound along the way.

+   Try looking up quotes about a favorite hobby or your profession.

+   Do you and your partner have an in-joke or saying between you?

+   An internet search for "short inspirational quotes" gives pretty wonderful results.

+   Sometimes the little things we are always reminding ourselves make good (or funny) banners, especially when you think about where the sign will be hung.

+   If you're still stuck, just write "DON'T GIVE UP" (even though you almost just did).

4

FAT QUARTER
PROJECTS

We *love* sewing for friends. It allows us to empty our houses and craft at the same time—plus, who on earth does not like presents?

The projects in this section are focused on things you can make with a fat quarter, but also make excellent gifts. There's a bike cap for the cyclist in your life (page 82), a basic potholder for a cook (page 60), and even an espadrilles template (page 75), although I'm certain you'll want to hold onto those for yourself.

When selecting a fabric for a gift, Spoonflower is perfect for complementing people's eclectic tastes. Whether you're sewing mittens (page 79) for a botanist, a soccer fan, or a cocktail enthusiast, there is probably a print in the Marketplace that reflects their interests. Or you can make your gifts even more personal by using a fabric you love from your own stash.

Featured fabric:
Lighthouse – Cream by lemonni

Quilted Potholders

Potholders add cheer and utility to any kitchen, especially when you choose bright fabrics and kitchen-themed prints. One fat quarter of cotton twill can easily yield two to three of either style, and you can add even more fun by mixing and matching designs. Try searching in the Spoonflower Marketplace for your favorite foods, your kitchen's colors, or just "cooking" to find a fabric that speaks to you.

MATERIALS + TOOLS

One fat quarter of basic cotton or cotton twill fabric

One 9-inch (23 cm) square of fusible cotton quilt batting

One 9-inch (23 cm) square of Insul-Bright

Basting spray

Basic sewing kit (see page 12)

½-inch (30.5 cm) wide masking tape or washi tape

Thread that matches the dominant color of your fabric

Pencil

One yard of coordinating ½-inch (1.3 cm) or 1-inch (2.5 cm) double-fold bias binding

Thread that matches your binding

5 inches (13 cm) of ribbon for loop to hang

Note: A 54-inch wide (137 cm) yard yields three square potholders—just triple the other materials above.

TO MAKE THE Square Potholder

1 Cut two 9-inch (23 cm) squares of fabric and one 9-inch (23 cm) square of batting. Sandwich the batting between the wrong sides of one square of fabric and one square of Insul-Bright, and press until it's adhered. Note, the batting won't stick to the Insul-Bright, but it *will* adhere to your iron or ironing surface. So use the Insul-Bright as a barrier.

2 Remove Insul-Bright, spray basting adhesive onto the cotton batting, then place the Insul-Bright back on top of it. Spray the wrong side of your second fabric square with spray adhesive, and place it face up on the Insul-Bright. Smooth it down with your hands until everything is pretty stuck together.

3 Using the ruler to guide you, tape diagonally in one direction across the square at 1½-inch (4 cm) intervals (photo A).

4 Line up the edge of your sewing machine's presser foot with one consistent side of the tape, and straight stitch along one side of each diagonal. A 3 mm stitch length is fine. Use a thread color that matches the background of your fabric design if you want the stitching to be less visible. Remove the tape.

5 Tape new lines perpendicular to the lines you've just stitched (photo A). Repeat, sewing along one side of the tape guides. Remove the tape. If necessary, trim edges of fabric so everything is the same size. Use scissors to round all four corners (photo B). You may want to trace around something curved you have on hand, like a spool of thread.

The following fabrics were used for this project: Spoonflower's Basic Cotton in Bouillabaise Plates, Bouillabaise, and Bouillabaise Dots by zesti

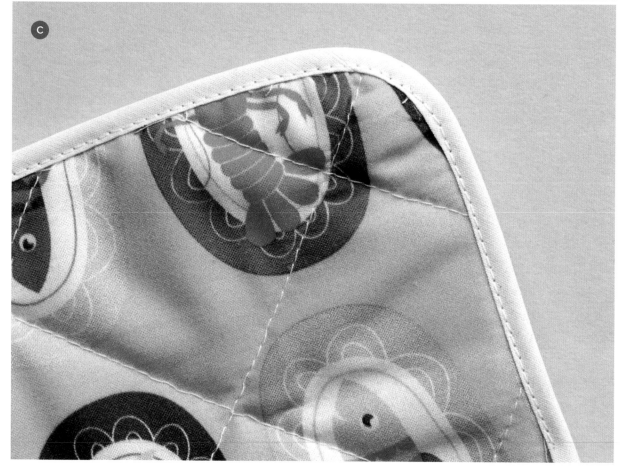

6   Unfold your bias binding and (right side down against fabric) line up the raw edge of the bias binding with the raw edge of the quilted square. Backstitch and then straight stitch in the fold of the binding.

7   When you reach the next rounded corner, tuck a loop of ribbon (I use a 4-inch [10 cm] length folded in half to 2 inches [5 cm] between the fabric and the bias binding). This is to create a loop to use to hang up the potholder later.

8   When you get all the way around, overlap the bias binding about 1 to 2 inches (2.5 to 5 cm), backstitch, and cut off excess.

9   Flip your square over and refold the bias binding around the raw edge, making sure to cover visible stitch line. Pin and then topstitch with a straight or zigzag stitch around the bias binding (photo C), backstitching when you reach the end.

Compass to create a 9-inch
(23 cm) circle

1 fat quarter of cotton twill
fabric

9-inch (23 cm) square of
fusible cotton quilt batting

9-inch (23 cm) square of Insul-
Bright

Basting spray

Basic sewing kit (see page 12)

½-inch (30.5 cm) wide masking
tape or washi tape

Thread that matches the
dominant color of your fabric

1 yard of coordinating ½-inch
(1.3 cm) or 1-inch (2.5 cm)
double-fold bias binding

Thread that matches your
binding

5 inches (13 cm) of ribbon for
loop to hang

Note: A 54-inch (137 cm)
wide yard yields two
round pocket potholders—
just double the other
materials above.

TO MAKE THE Circle Potholder with Pocket

1   Using a compass, draw a 9-inch (23 cm) circle on paper. Cut out.

2   Using this pattern, cut out three 9-inch (23 cm) circles of fabric. If you
have more than a fat quarter on hand, try a contrasting fabric for the
pocket (one circle) or reverse side of the potholder.

3   Cut a 9-inch (23 cm) circle of the fusible batting and 9-inch (23 cm) circle
of Insul-Bright. Sandwich the batting between the wrong sides of one
circle of fabric and the circle of Insul-Bright, and press until it's adhered.
Note, the batting won't stick to the Insul-Bright, but it *will* adhere to your
iron or ironing surface. So use the Insul-Bright as a barrier.

4   Remove Insul-Bright, spray basting adhesive onto the cotton batting,
then place the Insul-Bright back on top of it. Spray the wrong side of your
second fabric square with spray adhesive and place it face up on the
Insul-Bright. Smooth it down with your hands until everything is stuck
together.

5   Quilt as described above, or leave unquilted.

6   Sew the back side of the bias binding around the circle in the same
way described previously for the square potholder. Tuck a loop of ribbon
in where you want your potholder to hang.

7 Fold your circle pattern in half, and use it to cut out a half-circle of batting. With right side out, fold the pocket fabric in half and tuck the batting inside it like a taco. Press. Sew an 8-inch (20 cm) length of bias binding along the straight side of the folded pocket (photo A).

8 Flip the project over and line up the pocket piece raw edges to the circle's raw edges directly opposite the loop of ribbon. Refold the bias binding around the raw edges including the pocket piece, and pin. Topstitch around the entire circle, being very careful the pocket sides don't slip out as you stitch around them (photo B).

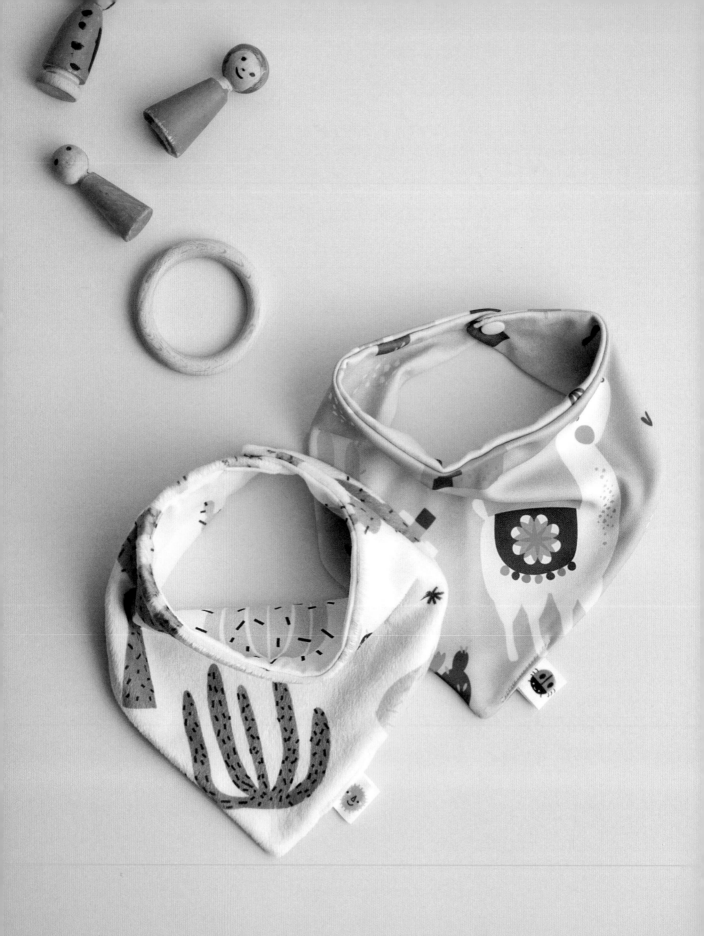

Dribble Bib

Bibs are a nice project for anyone planning on having or being around a new baby (and expectant seamstress moms: This is *the* most satisfying nesting project). They are a cinch to whip up and are a perfect way to use the last bits of your favorite fabrics from your stash. Don't make the mistake of thinking bibs are just for mealtime—more and more parents are finding a dribble bib (a bib worn to protect clothes from a drooly, teething baby) an essential part of their little one's daily wardrobe.

MATERIALS + TOOLS

1 fat quarter of fabric
Interfacing if using knit fabric
1-2 snaps
Snap fastener
Scanner and printer
Basic sewing kit (see page 12)

to design the fabric

1   To create a cut-and-sew design of your own, scan the pattern on page 170, print and design within the space. Then, scan at 150 DPI and upload to Spoonflower, making sure the straight grain is from the neckline of bib piece to the point. If you're designing using graphics software, make sure the test square is 1 inch (2.5 cm) when your design is 150 DPI.

to make the baby bib

1   Scan and enlarge the pattern on page 170 and then print. Cut out the pattern, place it along your folded fabric, and cut out one piece for the front and one for the back.

2   If necessary, iron interfacing on the wrong side of knit fabric. Notch the fabric at points marked on pattern—this is where you will leave the piece open to turn.

3   Place the bib pieces right sides together, lining up the notches, and pin. Backstitch. Next, sew ¼ inch (6 mm) from the seam, from one notch all around to the second. Notch all curves and clip the point of the bib, then turn and press.

4   Hand sew with an invisible stitch or simply topstitch the opening closed. We usually pop a tag in the opening (see page 26 for instructions to make your own fabric tags) (photo A).

The following fabrics were used for this project: Spoonflower's Organic Cotton Knit, Minky, and Performance Piqué, in Llamas Large by petite_circus and Boho Cactus by laurawrightstudio

5 Load up your snap fastener—if you have one—and insert snaps at the points shown on the pattern (about ½ inch [1.3 cm] from the seams). If you like, you can use Velcro instead of snaps, but be sure to stitch it down very securely, as babywear tends to get a lot of use (photo B).

Tips:

+ Dribble bibs are for everyday wear, but their main purpose is catching baby drool. You'll want something absorbent, which is why cotton fabric is perfect for this project. Try Spoonflower's Kona® Cotton, Cotton Poplin, Organic Sweet Pea Gauze™, or Organic Cotton Knit.

+ If you have more than a fat quarter on hand, consider using something soft that will double as a "barrier" fabric, like minky or fleece. Please note that if you're mixing cotton with poly fabrics, it's *very* important to prewash both fabrics to avoid mismatched shrinkage. In addition, if you're pairing a knit fabric with a woven, you'll find it useful to iron some interfacing on the back of the stretchier fabric to stabilize it.

+ Not sure where to start when shopping for a print? Try choosing motifs that reflect baby's nursery décor and colors. Our personal favorite bib theme is food—pizza and donuts never disappoint.

Pet Collar Bandana

We can't leave out our beloved four-legged family members when creating personalized bandanas. This variation on the project uses even less fabric, and you can adjust the pattern easily to accommodate pups of all sizes.

MATERIALS + TOOLS
1 fat quarter of cotton poplin
Basic sewing kit (see page 12)
Scanner and printer

1   Scan and enlarge the pattern piece on page 171 to desired size (Olive, the model in the photograph, is wearing the template enlarged to 135%), print, and cut out.

2   Fold the fabric on the cross grain and cut the pattern piece on the fold.

3   Open up and place right side down. Fold in, and press the two shorter parallel sides ¼ inch (6 mm), and then fold and press another ⅜ inch (1 cm). Topstitch ¼ inch (6 mm) from the edge to hem (photo A).

4   Fold in half with right sides together, lining up bandana points. On just the two sides of the points (not the hemmed edges), sew with a ¼-inch (6 mm) seam. Clip the point, and turn through one of the hemmed openings. Press.

5   Use a ruler and a washable pen to draw a line from the top of the point of one side to the other, and topstitch to create a casing for a collar, then topstitch around the point of the bandana ¼ inch (6 mm) from seam.

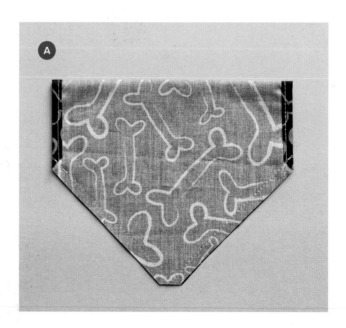

The following fabric was used for this project: Spoonflower's Cotton Poplin in Give a Dog a Bone by shindigdesignstudio

Jessica Prout of littlearrowdesign

Based in Richmond, Virginia, designer Jessica Prout aka littlearrowdesign has been a long-time Spoonflower favorite, with her range of woodland silhouettes, illustrated sweets, and fun typography.

The combination of Jessica's love for fabric and her husband's background as a graphic designer led her to try designing. Needless to say, she was instantly hooked: Her littlearrowdesign shop now offers more than five thousand designs.

Whether you're thinking about designing your own fabric or you have a project in mind for a unique pattern that channels your aesthetic, there's never a better time to get started. Jessica's advice: "Trust yourself and your ability to succeed through hard work and dedication."

The Fabrics

The expert use of color is noticeable in littlearrowdesign's fabrics and something that you can use to inspire color combinations in projects of your own. Geometrics like the Navy Aztec and Modern Aztec balance each other beautifully in their color schemes. Also, don't be afraid to mix and match different patterns like Falling Triangles and Buffalo Aztec—the results might surprise you!

Some insight from Jessica at littlearrowdesign on her work:

How do you feel when you're working on projects?
"Happy. I love designing, and being able to create daily is something that I am very grateful for."

When did you fall in love with design?
"I have always had a passion for creating, but it wasn't until after my first daughter was born and I stopped working full time, that I started pattern design. My passion and call to create is so strong, it is hard to think there was ever a time when I didn't do it at all."

The secret to a strong collection is . . .
"Choosing a strong color palette, a variety of scale, and making some basic blender fabrics that coordinate with your hero print."

Who or what influences or inspires your work and why?
"I am most definitely inspired by all things nature and wildlife, but I also love to do illustrations of different objects that I find fun & interesting."

Featured littlearrowdesign fabrics, from left (top to bottom), to right (top to bottom):
Navy Aztec, Modern Aztec – Tan & Navy, Falling Triangle – Dusty Blue, Multi Bear with Gold,
Buffalo Aztec – Distressed Navy; border design Fletching Arrows – Young and Brave with Navy

Espadrilles

Finding the espadrille soles hanging in our local fabric store was a life-changing event. Making your own shoes can feel so daunting and seems to require a pile of equipment and knowledge most of us don't have. However, these shoes can be made with regular fabric and ordinary tools. And we promise, once you've tried making these, you're going to want to make them as gifts for everyone you know!

If you want to design the fabric yourself, use the espadrille pattern on page 172 as a template. Print out several copies and draw, paint, or collage within the lines (and maybe a bit outside of the lines), then scan at 150 DPI and upload to Spoonflower. Choose "mirror" as the repeat and order a fat quarter of linen cotton canvas. Congratulations, you've just made a cut-and-sew pattern!

MATERIALS + TOOLS

Scanner and printer

1 fat quarter of linen cotton canvas in your shoe design

1 fat quarter of coordinating lining fabric

1 skein of embroidery floss in a coordinating color

A sharp embroidery needle or chenille needle

Basic sewing kit (see page 12)

Espadrille soles (found online or at larger craft stores)

The following fabric was used for this project: Spoonflower's Linen Cotton Canvas in Woven Stripe Neutral by holli_zollinger

1   Enlarge the pattern on page 172 and print. Cut out two pattern pieces of outer fabric (left and right shoes) and mirror pieces of lining fabric. Notch fabric at points noted in the pattern and then mark left and right shoe pieces so you don't mix them up.

2   Line up outer and inner toe pieces of one shoe, right sides together. Beginning at notch A, sew a ⅜-inch (1 cm) seam around all sides until you reach notch B. This should leave a 1¼-inch (3 cm) space for turning. Clip the fabric bulk from the corners and curved edges and turn right side out. Tuck the ⅜-inch (1 cm) seam of the opening inside and press.

3   Line up the outer and inner heel pieces of one shoe, right sides together. Beginning at notch A, sew a ⅜-inch (1 cm) seam around all sides until you reach notch B. This should leave a 1¼-inch (3 cm) space for turning. Clip the fabric bulk from the corners and turn right side out. Tuck the ⅜-inch (1 cm) seam of opening inside and press. Then repeat all steps with opposite shoe.

4   Next, we're going to pin them to the soles. Line up the center of the left heel piece with the back center of the left sole. Stick straight pins through the front side of the piece through both layers of fabric into the sole about ⅜ inch (1 cm) from the bottom edge. Pin generously all around the perimeter until you've pinned the heel piece to the shoe—the pieces should end at roughly the same points on both sides, near your arches.

Don't pin the fabric very taut around the front of the shoe; add lots of pins instead, and almost gather the fabric a tiny bit—doing this gives your toes some wiggle room (photo A).

5   Begin at one side of the pinned piece and hand sew onto the sole with a blanket stitch. Espadrille soles are soft enough to stick a needle through, and you shouldn't have any trouble. When you sew through the sole, angle your needle 45 degrees from the top to the side.

6   Align the toe piece onto the toe of the sole, and pin in the same way you did for the heel, adjusting it so that it overlaps each of the sides you've stitched down about ¾ inch (2 cm). Once pinned in place, blanket stitch in the same way as above (photo B).

7   To finish, hand stitch with a few decorative topstitches where the toe piece overlaps the heel piece to connect them (photo B).

Tip:

+   Commercial espadrille soles will come with a graded pattern so you can make them exactly your size. However, after making a few pairs, we found ourselves tweaking the pattern here and there for a better fit. The template on page 172 is made for a women's size 8 or 9, but you can enlarge or reduce the template with your printer for different sizes.

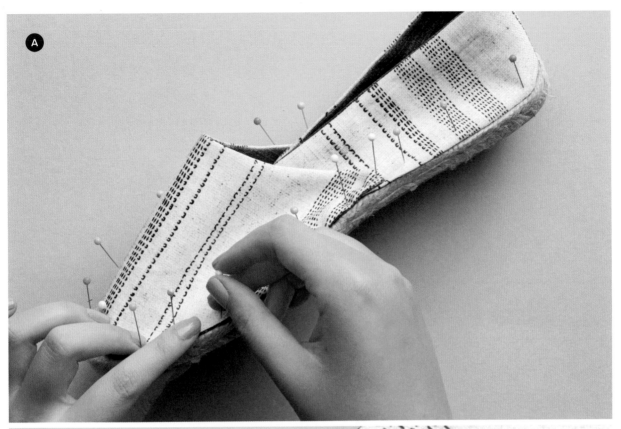

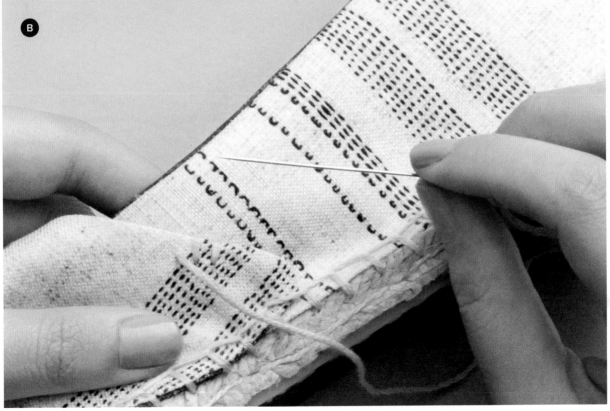

Fleece Mittens

This is another fat quarter project you can whip up in an hour. These mittens are ideal for whenever you have fleece or even old sweaters and sweatshirts you've saved to upcycle. You just need one 28-inch (71 cm) by 18-inch (46 cm) swath of a thick stretchy fabric, your sewing machine, and that's it. They make excellent stocking stuffers—and we've provided three sizes of the pattern pieces (page 174), so you can have your whole family's hands covered. Each mitten is made of an outer fabric, lining, and cuff. You can make them with just one fat quarter of Spoonflower's Fleece, or mix and match stretchy fleeces from your stash.

MATERIALS + TOOLS

One fat quarter of fleece fabric
Scanner and printer
Basic sewing kit (see page 12),
   including a machine that
   can sew a zigzag stitch
Serger (optional, and very
   helpful)

1   Enlarge the pattern on page 174 and print. Cut out two of each pattern piece, mirrored. Fleece can be finicky to work with, so as you construct these, always generously pin and go slowly to make sure you're not stretching the fabric. If you have a serger, it will make sewing these much easier.

2   Begin with two palm pieces. With right sides of the fabric together, line up the dots, and pin. Backstitch, and sew a ¼-inch (6 mm) seam from dot to dot along the curvy line of the palm (photo A). Notch the fabric along the curve.

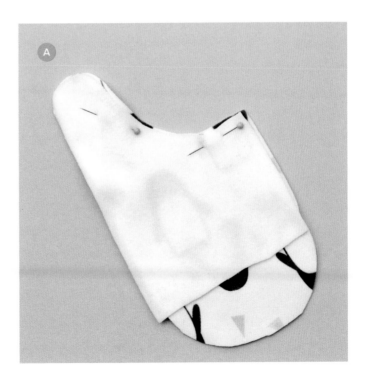

The following fabric was used for this project: Spoonflower's Fleece in Ice Cold Penguins – White by papercanoefabricshop

3   Open the two palm pieces away from each other—you will then have a horseshoe shape like the back piece, with the thumb now in the center. Pin the thumb out of the way of the side seams. With right sides of fabric together, pin the back piece to the palm piece, leaving the bottom open (photo B). Backstitch and sew a ⅜-inch (1 cm) seam from one side to the other.

4   Repeat above steps with second glove. Turn both gloves right side out.

5   Take one of the cuff rectangles and match up the raw edges of the two longer sides, right sides of the fabric facing out. Straight stitch ⅜ inch (1 cm) along this side to create a little tube of fabric.

6   Slide the glove right side out into the cuff tube, aligning the open bottom of the glove to the open end of the cuff (photo C). Sew this seam with a zigzag stitch (or continue using your serger). Roll up the bottom cuff up twice until it covers this seam. Repeat with opposite mitten.

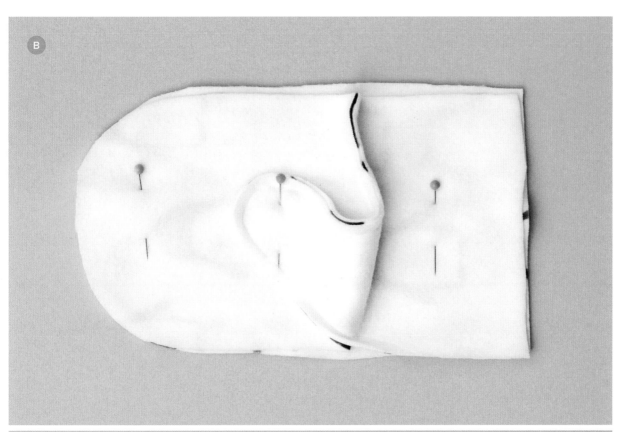

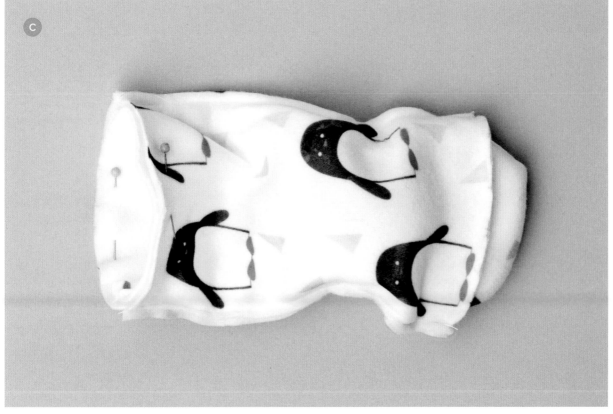

Bike Cap

This project works best with a light woven outer fabric like cotton poplin and a fabric with moisture-wicking properties for the lining like performance piqué. (Prewash both fabrics first to avoid mismatched shrinkage.) However, if you only have a 28-inch (71 cm) by 18-inch (46 cm) fat quarter of any fabric, that's enough to complete a hat.

This pattern is very versatile and once you get familiar with the basic construction you can do all kinds of things with it. For instance, we've cut apart plastic IKEA shopping totes for hats, added cat ears for children's party favors, sewed them using upholstery fabric, recycled sweaters, oilcloths, and more. Each pattern piece is a quarter of the hat and less than an 8-inch (20 cm) square, so you can even use a split yard of Spoonflower fabric or a pile of swatches and make a patchwork-y hat with four (or more) different prints!

MATERIALS + TOOLS

1 fat quarter of cotton poplin fabric

1 fat quarter of lightweight interfacing

Plastic for inside the brim— try cutting it from a recycled and washed plastic takeout container (you could use heavyweight interfacing instead)

Basic sewing kit (see page 12)

1   Iron your interfacing onto the wrong side of the fabric, and cut out the pattern pieces using the guide on page 176. The pattern uses a ¼-inch (6 mm) seam allowance. Cut the piece for inside the brim out of plastic— you can use a takeout box or any plastic container you've washed and recycled.

2   Take the two crescent-shaped brim pieces, right sides facing down, and fold the raw edge of the straighter sides toward you ¼ inch (6 mm) and press. With right sides of fabric together, stitch a ¼-inch (6 mm) seam along the curvier side of the two brim pieces. Notch the fabric along curves and clip the corners. Turn right side out (the seam you pressed before sewing will fold in at the opening), and press. Work the plastic piece into the opening (photo A).

3   Fold each crown piece in half (right side of fabric inward) so that the points align, and pin. Stitch with a ¼-inch (6 mm) seam from fold to top of point. Repeat for all eight crown pieces. Notch the fabric on these curved seams, and press seam open.

4   Pin two of the outer crown pieces with right sides together along one curve, with points aligning. Stitch a ¼-inch (6 mm) seam. Repeat with the next two outer crown pieces. Notch the curved seams, and press seam open.

The following fabric was used for this project: Spoonflower's Cotton Poplin Ultra in Gold Paint Blobs on Cream by jenlats

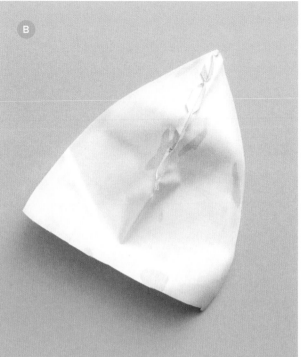

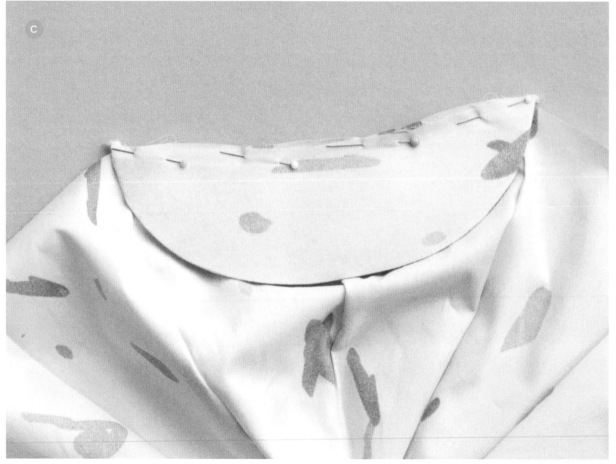

5   Pin these two pieces (right side of fabric together) along remaining raw edges of curved sides and stitch with a ¼-inch (6 mm) seam (photo B). Notch the seam along the curve, and press open. This is the outer crown of your cap. It will have four panels total and kind of look like a beanie— or a bike cap without a brim! Repeat these steps for the crown pieces of lining.

6   Arrange the crown lining right side out and so that one panel is centered in front of you. Pin the straighter side of the cap brim to the raw edge against the right side of lining fabric, centered to this panel, and baste the brim to the lining (photo C). Pop the outer crown around the lining crown (right sides of fabric together) and pin together all around the base of the hat.

7   Mark a 2-inch (5 cm) opening opposite where you've basted the brim— you'll leave this open to turn the cap—backstitch, and sew a ¼-inch (6 mm) seam around the base until you reach the other side of your 2-inch (5 cm) mark. Turn the cap right side out—you'll need to bend the brim a little to ease it through the opening. Topstitch the opening at the back of the cap closed.

8   Measure the head of whomever the cap is for and subtract an inch (2.5 cm). Cut your elastic to this measurement. Loop the elastic piece and overlap the ends about ½ inch (1.3 cm) and stitch back and forth over them to connect. Pin this loop of elastic to the lining side of the perimeter of the cap. When you get to the back panel, stretch the elastic as you pin to gather it. Using a zigzag stitch, sew the elastic to the bottom of the hat around its perimeter.

Tip:
+   Sew a covered button (see page 22) in a matching fabric at the top of the crown to hide any wonkiness where all the seams merge.

Travel Bag

These boxy, zippered bags are large enough to hold a pair of shoes and make great gifts for your world-traveling (or maybe just gym-going) friends. Heavy twill or canvas makes them sturdy enough to last a while, and our favorite trick of hiding inner seams with bias binding means no lining is necessary.

MATERIALS + TOOLS

18-inch (46 cm) by 28-inch (71 cm) piece of heavy cotton twill fabric

15-inch (38 cm) nylon closed zipper

6 inches (15 cm) of ¾-inch (2 cm) cotton twill tape

1 yard (91 cm) of ½-inch (1.3 cm) double-fold bias binding

Basic sewing kit (see page 12)

Zipper foot for your machine

Tip:

+ Try making pencil cases, proper Dopp kits, square makeup travel bags, and more.

1 Cut one 2-inch (5 cm) by 8-inch (20 cm) strip, and one 16-inch (40.5 cm) by 22-inch (59 cm) rectangle of fabric.

2 To make the handle, fold the long sides of the strip to the wrong side ¼-inch (6 mm), and press. Fold the entire piece in half lengthwise and press. Topstitch the long edges and set aside.

3 Lay the fabric right side up. Take the zipper and place it face down along one of the 16-inch (40.5 cm) sides, centered and lined up with raw edge (photo A). Use your machine's zipper foot to sew the zipper to the fabric with a ¼-inch (6 mm) seam. Bring the zipper's opposite side over to the opposite 16-inch side (40.5 cm), line up edges, and sew. You'll now have a big tube of fabric making a 16-inch (40.5 cm) by 12-inch (30.5 cm) rectangle, with wrong side of fabric visible. Center the zipper within the rectangle and press the sides of the fabric; avoid pressing the zipper directly.

4 Open the zipper a few inches (photo B). Cut the cotton twill tape piece in two equal pieces and fold each in half. Sandwich these between the fabric opening in the middle, overtop the zipper, raw edges aligned. Pin in place. Repeat on opposite open side.

5 Take the handle piece and pin each end between the two layers of fabric, 3 inches (7.5 cm) from each side of the zipper as shown. Baste this edge closed, then baste opposite the open side closed (photo B).

6 Measure and cut a 2-inch (5 cm) square from each corner, taking care not to cut the handle inside the bag. Cut two 8½-inch (21.5 cm) pieces of the bias binding. Unfold one side of the bias binding and line up with one side of the fabric you've just basted (photo C). Straight stitch along the fold,

The following fabric was used for this project: Spoonflower's Linen Cotton in By The Sea – Waves by lemonni

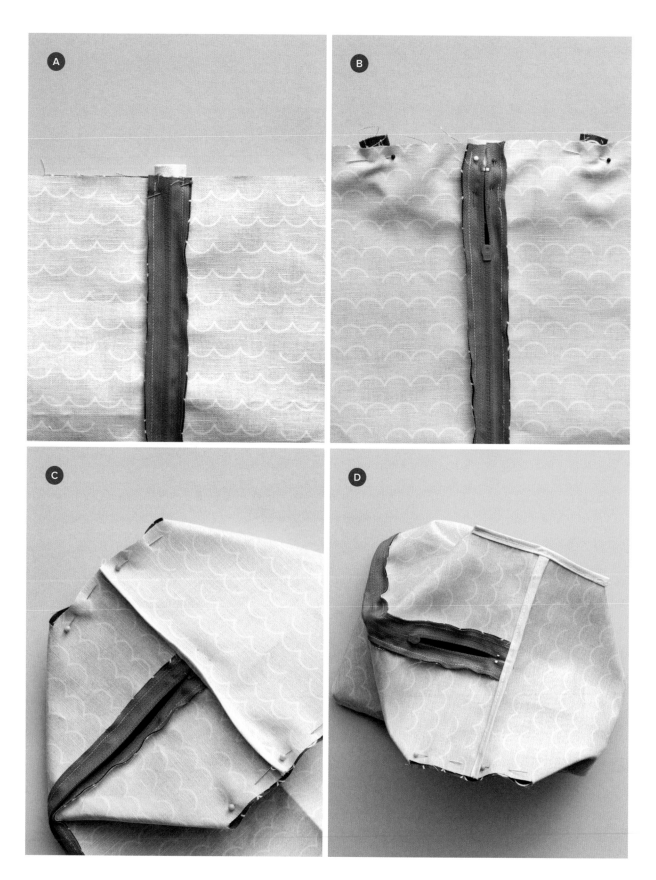

going carefully over the zipper and cotton twill tape. Fold the bias binding over the seam and topstitch the opposite side to bind the seam. Repeat with second basted seam.

7   Open up one of the cut-out corners, and bring the bias tape seam to the end of the fabric diagonally across from it, aligning raw edges and creating a new seam of about 4 inches (10 cm). Sew the bias binding around this seam in the same way as above (photo D). Repeat for remaining three corner openings. Turn right side out, and you've finished.

Tip:

Much like a recipe, you can adjust the dimensions given to customize the bag's size. Just keep these things in mind:

+   The zipper length should be 1 inch (2.5 cm) less than the shorter side of your rectangle.

+   Make a longer handle than you need and then, while pinning it in, adjust the length until it suits you.

+   The bit you clip from the corners should always be a perfect square.

Pop-Up Puppets

You don't need a lot of fabric to make these vintage-inspired puppets. One fat quarter is easily enough for three, so if you're looking for a project to put a dent in your scrap bag, this is it. You can mix and match various weights and types of fabrics: Just try to collect pieces larger than an 8-inch (20 cm) square. Wooden dowels and dowel caps are available at most larger craft stores and online. These make such sweet gifts for the little ones in your life and once you've finished, find the Doorway Puppet Theater on page 161 to learn how to sew a stage for your creations.

MATERIALS + TOOLS

Basic sewing kit (see page 12)
1 fat quarter of lightweight cotton fabric
1 sheet of poster board
X-Acto knife or razor blade
Glue gun
Three 12-inch (30.5 cm) wooden dowels, ¼-inch (6 mm) diameter
Three wooden dowel caps, 1¼-inch (3 cm) diameter with ½-inch (1.3 cm) hole
Three wooden dowel caps, ¾-inch (2 cm) diameter with ¼-inch (6 mm) hole
Sandpaper
Fine-tipped paint markers in black, white, and pink or red
Acrylic paint
Scrap of black felt (for cat ears)
Yarn or embroidery floss in any color (for hair)
25 inches (63.5 cm) of ribbon (optional for embellishment)
Buttons (optional for embellishment)
Embroidery tools (optional for embellishment)
Scanner and printer

1 Scan the cone template on page 179 and print. Cut out the template, trace three copies onto poster board, and cut out with an X-Acto knife.

2 Add ½-inch (1.3 cm) seam allowance to the cone template, and cut three from your fabric.

3 Place one of the fabric pieces face down, and place one of the pieces of poster board on top of it, centered so there is ½ inch (1.3 cm) of fabric around all sides (photo A). Fold this extra fabric over and hot glue it to the back of the poster board.

4 Roll paper into a cone shape and glue closed along one side with hot glue. Leave a hole at the bottom of your cone larger than ¼ inch (6 mm). Repeat to make three cones.

5 Scan the puppet body pattern on page 178 and print. Cut six of the pattern from your fabric. If using different fabrics, cut out the pieces in pairs.

6 Fold the bottom of each puppet body piece ¼ inch (6 mm) to the wrong side, press, and topstitch. With right sides together, line up two body pieces and straight stitch with a ¼-inch (6 mm) seam around the sides and arms, leaving the top and bottom open. Clip the curved edges and turn right side out (photo B). Repeat with next two pairs of body pieces. If desired, decorate one side of the puppet bodies with buttons or with embroidery.

The following fabrics were used for this project: Spoonflower's Kona® Cotton in Autumn in the Woods and Autumn in the Woods – Ivory by shopcabin, and Solid Linen Neutral by nouveau_bohemian

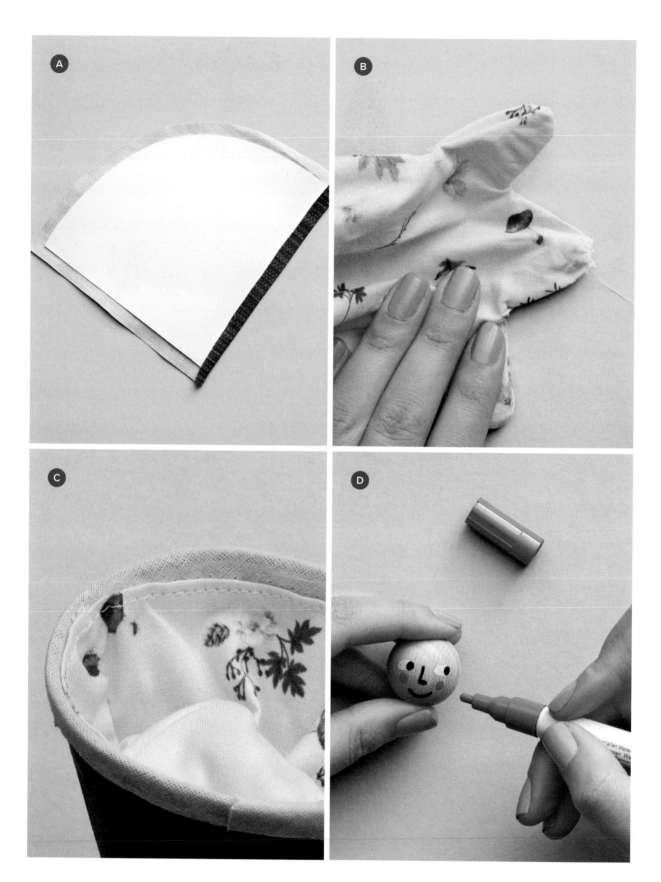

7 Tuck one puppet body into the top of a cone, with the bottom edge of puppet lined up wrong side against the inside of cone, 1 inch (2.5 cm) down from top. Carefully glue the fabric to the inner side of cone with hot glue (photo C).

8 Prime the paint markers by shaking and pressing the tip against scrap paper until ink flows. Paint one large dowel cap black for the cat. Mix paint for the other two puppet heads and paint the other two dowel caps, then set aside and let dry completely. Once dry, use the paint markers to draw faces. Make sure the hole in the dowel caps is at the bottom—this is the puppet's neck.

9 Use the white paint or marker to make two solid ovals, then black dots inside them, with round circles in pink underneath for rosy cheeks. Draw an L for a nose and a little semi-circle for a mouth—easy and cute (photo D).

10 Make a 6-inch (15 cm) long bundle of yarn (or just use an entire skein of embroidery floss) and tie in the center. Glue to the top of puppet heads for hair, then trim to length desired. You can also gather into a ponytail, braid it, or glue a bit to the face for bangs.

11 Once the black dowel cap is completely dry, draw a cat face on it with the paint markers. Draw two white solid ovals; add black dots and pink cheeks. Then use the white paint marker to make an X and connect the top of the X with a line for the cat's mouth. Cut two small triangles from the felt and hot glue to the top of the cat head.

12 Stick one of the dowels through the bottom of a cone. Drop a bit of hot glue into one of the smaller dowel caps and push the bottom of the dowel into the hole.

13 Hand baste the top of the puppet body loosely and pull thread to gather closed. Drop a bit of hot glue into the hole of one of the painted dowel caps, and then use the opposite dowel end to push the fabric into the hole. Repeat for remaining puppets. If you like, glue ribbon or ric rac around the top of the cone, and otherwise embellish as you like. All done!

Featured fabrics, from top left to bottom: Tropical Leaves by willowlanetextiles, Tooth Fairy by susiprint, Fishy by elliewhittaker, Flower Cocktail by peacoquettedesigns, Llamas Large by petite_circus, Bebe Mudcloth by holli_zollinger, Blackbirds on Peach by anda, Urban Garden Banana Palm by holli_zollinger, Bird Wings by pencilmein, Blush Splatter by holli_zollinger, Wink and Smile by haleeholland, Dotted Stroke by primuspattern, Crane Deco – Peach by lemonni, Gold Paint Blobs on Cream by jenlats, Watercolor Leaves by shopcabin, Seaweed Beach by anda, Handmade Tags by anda, Sumi Splash by frumafar, and Sail Away and Mudcloth Gray by willowlanetextiles

5
ONE-YARD PROJECTS

In the last section, we sewed gifts from fat quarters, because making and giving handmade presents can be the most fun. Now it's time to step it up a bit with a few simple projects that use a yard of fabric! The projects in this section are sure to brighten up your home in fun and clever ways. Your little ones will be thrilled when you use our tutorial for making a pile of colorful, handmade dress-up clothes, complete with hats and crowns. Plus, the quiet you'll inherit while they are busy imagining will give you plenty of time to make beautiful envelope pillows for your couch or a handy knitting caddy for organizing yarn, magazines, and more! Each of these projects can be made from your favorite fabrics or original patterns that you design, resulting in projects that are wonderfully unique.

There is so much to be made from that favorite yard of fabric you have been hoarding in your stash, and we can't wait to see what you create! Let's get started.

Featured fabrics: Wildflower Seeds
Neutral by holli_zollinger, Deer
Hide by willowlanetextiles, Protea
Neutral by holli_zollinger

School Chart Wall Hanging

If you're like some of us, you may have a mild vintage shopping addiction. We love searching for and collecting everything from old-school chart posters of out-of-date maps, botanical illustrations, combustion engine diagrams, and snake skeleton illustrations. Maybe you've even spent time buying or bidding on diagrams of the water cycle or posters detailing the songbirds of northern Germany. Whatever the design, these unique wall hangings are full of character and can add beauty and interest to any space.

This affection for these gorgeous charts got us thinking that they couldn't be too difficult to make ourselves! Just think of how fun it would be to have your own one-of-a-kind homemade school chart to adorn your walls, no online bidding required.

MATERIALS + TOOLS

1 yard (91 cm) of linen cotton canvas fabric with one large format design. Upload the design so it is oriented with the sides parallel to the straight grain (sideways) and leave a few inches around the sides of your design for hemming

Basic sewing kit (see page 12)

Ruler

Pencil

Triangle (optional for cutting rectangles)

Four pieces of ¾-inch (2 cm) diameter and 36-inch (91 cm) long wooden half-round moulding

Wood glue

Clamps

Two thumbtacks

About 30 inches (76 cm) of baker's twine (if you want the poster to hang more invisibly, use fishing line)

to design the fabric

1 To get started, design a large format image for your fabric. Vector images are nice for larger prints because you can create a smaller file and then adjust the actual size when uploading to Spoonflower, without loss of image quality. Another way to get a nice big image is to scan at a high resolution such as 600 DPI, or you can just work large in Photoshop and keep an eye on your file size (Spoonflower's limit is 40 MB). If you're not working in a vector format, remember your final .jpg image only needs to be 150 DPI.

2 For this poster we knew we wanted to do something inspired by classroom décor, and decided on mathematics as a theme. So, we painted 100 circles on white paper in a 10 x 10 grid, to demonstrate the decimal relationship between 100, 10, and 1. Using a primary color palette of blue, red, and yellow kept it graphic and fun—but we couldn't resist drawing smiles on every dot with a black paint marker. Simple, minimal, and really easy.

3 As far as themes go, the sky really is the limit. If you're making a poster for home use only, try searching through vintage children's textbooks from the thrift store for images to scan. (Never use found images commercially unless you are positive you're not violating any copyright laws!) You can also search online for royalty-free images, although designing something

The following fabric was used for this project: Spoonflower's Linen Cotton Canvas in 100 Smiling Dots School Chart by anda

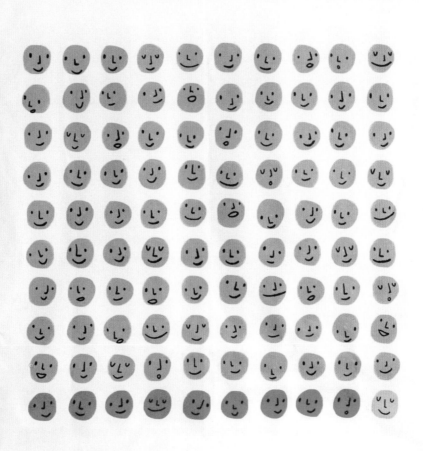

yourself from scratch is the most fun. Try drawing an entire page of local wildflowers, creating an illustrated alphabet, or your own food pyramid/ nutritional chart. Just flipping through a children's picture encyclopedia will provide loads of inspiration.

to make the school chart wall hanging

1   Trim off selvage and excess from fabric, then use a ruler and triangle to cut fabric into a 36-inch (91 cm) wide rectangle. (The height can be anything you like—as long as it fits on your wall!)

2   Press the rectangle to remove all folds and wrinkles. Lay the fabric flat, wrong side up, then fold left and right sides over ½ inch (1.3 cm) and press. Fold again ¾ inch (2 cm), and press. Pin in place and topstitch ½ inch (1.3 cm) from seam to hem each side.

3   With a pencil, mark the center of the bottom of the fabric, and the center of one piece of half round moulding. Apply a thin line of wood glue to the flat side of the moulding and line up the marks (photo A). Apply glue to the flat side of a second piece of moulding and sandwich them together, creating a whole round wooden dowel along the bottom edge of your wall hanging.

4   Repeat these steps for the top with the two remaining wood half rounds. Use clamps to hold together and let the glue dry. Wood glue takes an hour to dry, but twenty-four hours to cure, and you should really keep the wood clamped together a full day to ensure the longevity of your project.

5   Once the wood glue is cured, measure about 8 inches (20 cm) from each end of the top dowel and press a thumbtack into the back. Loop twine to each thumbtack (this method keeps the string in place), trim excess, and hang!

Travel Playmat

Using a million colors is fun, especially for kids' stuff, but sometimes your eyes need a break. For this travel playmat we decided to work in a limited palette and create something more minimal (perfect for a nursery that has a specific color scheme). The best part? Getting the look is easy! This is a simple project to sew once you've designed your playmat image since you're really just making an enormous potholder.

MATERIALS + TOOLS

7-inch (18 cm) by 9-inch (23 cm) sheet of paper

Paint and paint markers in black, white, and one secondary color

An inexpensive 1-inch (2.5 cm) flat paintbrush

Colored construction paper in a color matching your secondary paint color

Pencils and scrap paper

One 56-inch (142 cm) wide yard of organic cotton knit fabric, half of playmat design and half of a coordinating print

1 extra fat quarter of the coordinating print you chose above (for pocket)

72 inches (183 cm) of 1-inch (2.5 cm) double-fold bias binding, also in cotton knit fabric

28-inch (71 cm) by 36-inch (91 cm) piece of fusible quilt batting

4 feet of 1-inch (2.5 cm) cotton twill tape

Basic sewing kit (see page 12)

The following fabric was used for this project: Spoonflower's Organic Cotton Knit in Minimal Blue Playmat and Tiny Blue Trees by anda

to design your fabric

Note: For best results, read through these steps and sketch out your design loosely on scrap paper first.

1   Use your black paint and paintbrush to make a big, loose, looping shape that fills the page. Then take the white paint marker and draw a dotted line down the middle of it to create the road.

2   Now draw or cut rectangles of the colored construction paper for the buildings, and glue along the road to create the town. Add details to these buildings with the paint markers.

3   Use paint to add details like trees and lakes—since we're going for a minimal look, a tree can just be a circle with a trunk or a triangle. Keep it simple!

4   Scan vertically at 600 DPI and upload to Spoonflower. A 7-inch (18 cm) by 9-inch (23 cm) image scanned at 600 DPI will allow you to print a 28-inch (71 cm) by 36-inch (91 cm) design at 150 DPI, which just so happens to equal a half yard of organic cotton knit!

Tip:

+   Don't have the time or energy to physically draw your design? Just use a drawing app like Procreate to get your image set without needing to paint a thing!

to make the playmat

1   Cut the yard of fabric into two equal 28-inch (71 cm) by 36-inch (91 cm) rectangles, one of the mat image and one for the backing. Use a triangle, ruler, and rotary cutter to make sure it is straight.

2   Cut the batting to exactly the same size as the fabric pieces, sandwich between them with right sides out, pin, and press. See what we meant when we said earlier that this is just a giant potholder? The fusible batting keeps everything in place and makes quilting unnecessary. You could, if desired, hand or machine quilt at this point. Otherwise, move on to next step.

3   Sew the bias tape around your project. Open up the bias tape and pin the raw edge to the seam on the back of your mat (photo A). Straight stitch, stopping ⅛ inch (1 cm) from each corner to pivot and miter the corner.

4   Fold your bias tape up and to the right to make a 90-degree angle. Use your finger to press it. Then, fold your tape straight out to the left and line up with the raw edge of the next side. Starting ⅗ inch (1.5 cm) from corner, resume sewing, backstitch, and then sew along this edge (photo B).

5   When you get back to the beginning, overlap the bias tape about 1 inch (2.5 cm). Fold the tape around the edges of the mat to the front, making sure the bias tape is folded under, neatly press, and pin in place. Topstitch ¼ inch (6 mm) from the edge around the mat. That's it! Is that not the easiest thing? It's really almost too easy. If you agree, try making the variation on page 106 that includes a pocket that'll let you carry a few toys or dolls when you fold it up.

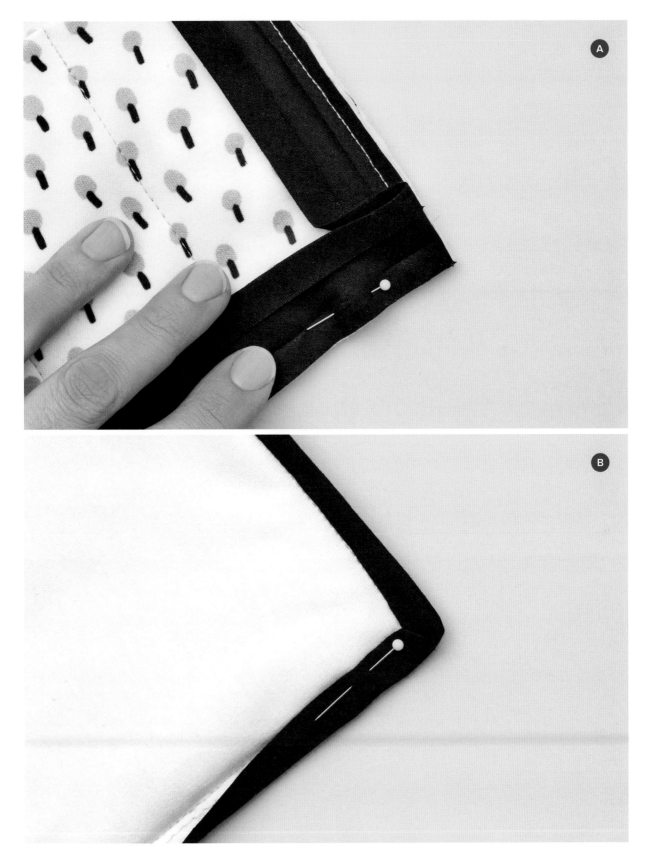

Playmat with Pocket

1   Design and upload a playmat image as above, but order an extra fat quarter of your backing print as well. Cut out the two playmat pieces and fusible interfacing, and set aside.

2   Cut the fat quarter into a 28-inch (71 cm) by 10-inch (25 cm) rectangle and cut the cotton twill tape into four 12-inch lengths (30.5 cm).

3   Take the larger rectangle of fabric and fold it lengthwise and press. Pin the raw seams lined up to the bottom (28-inch [71 cm] side) of the mat backing fabric and baste ⅛ inch (3 mm) from edges. Measure 3 inches (7.5 cm) from one side of the pocket and mark a straight line from top of pocket to bottom. Mark the pocket at 2-inch (5 cm) intervals until you reach the other side (the last mark will be 3 inch (7.5 cm) from edge). Topstitch these lines to create 10 mini pockets.

4   Pin the ends of two of the cotton twill tape lengths to the top raw edge of the backing fabric (the side opposite the pocket), 6 inches (15 cm) from one corner. Pin the other two pieces 6 inches (15 cm) from the opposite top corner. Stitch into place. These will be the ties to keep the playmat closed when rolled up for traveling.

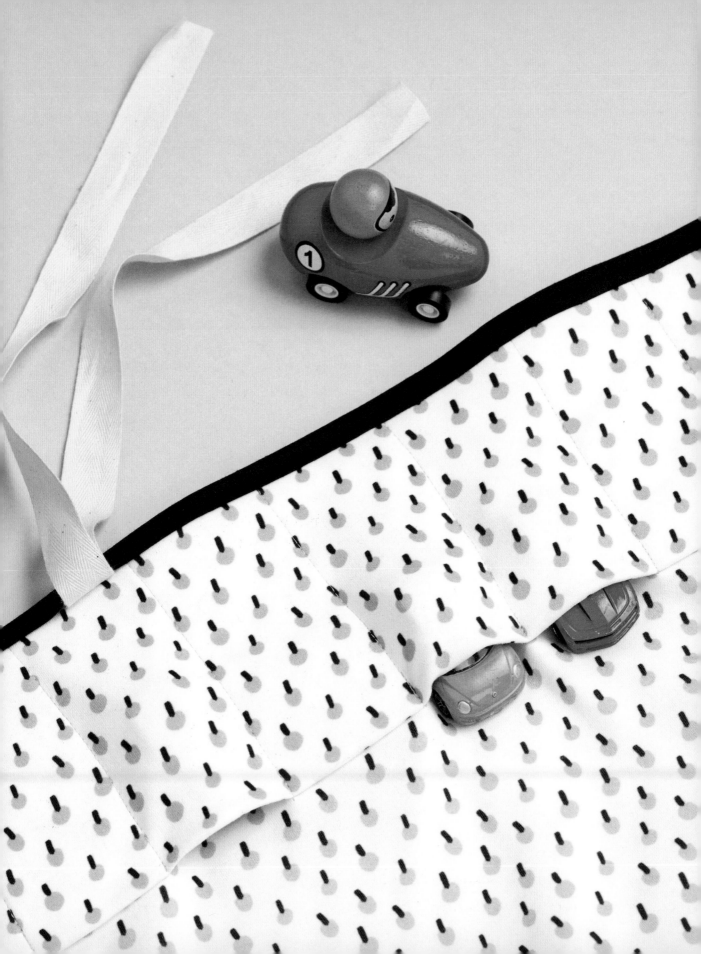

Basic Envelope Pillow

We're pretty certain you can never have too many pillows. There's nothing like a sofa piled high with colorful cushions in mixed and contrasting prints. Envelope pillows are the most basic form of pillow and are really just a folded-up rectangle with four straight lines of stitching. These pillows are also great as a first project when teaching kids (or adults) to sew. Because of its simplicity, you can make yourself a sofa full of pillows in an afternoon if you have the materials on hand.

MATERIALS + TOOLS

(FOR ONE SQUARE 20-INCH (51 CM) PILLOW)

1 yard (91 cm) of woven fabric—try linen cotton canvas, lightweight cotton twill, or velvet

82 inches (2 m) of piping (see page 21 if you want to make your own)

Basic sewing kit (see page 12)

Zipper foot

20-inch (51 cm) square pillow insert

Featured fabrics: Vintage Moroccan – Bone by littlearrowdesign, Mosaic Tile Sandstone, Bebe Mudcloth, and Seville Quilt White by holli_zollinger

The following fabric was used for this project: Spoonflower's Lightweight Cotton Twill in Vintage Moroccan – Bone by littlearrowdesign

1 Cut one 20-inch (51 cm) square from your yard of fabric for the front and two 20-inch (51 cm) by 14-inch (35.5 cm) pieces for the back.

2 On each back piece, fold one 20-inch (51 cm) side to the wrong side of the fabric ¼ inch (6 mm), and press. Fold again 1 inch (2.5 cm) and press. Topstitch a ⅞-inch (2 cm) seam to hem.

3 Place the front square face up in front of you and pin the piping around the raw edges, with the cording about ⅜ inch (1 cm) from the edge. Start pinning in the middle of one side rather than at a corner, and begin with an inch (2.5 cm) or so of the piping hanging off the edge of the fabric. At the corners, curve the piping and clip it (careful not to cut through to cording).

4 When you reach the point where you started pinning, overlap the piping a tiny bit and let its end run off the edge of the fabric (photo A). Baste piping around the entire perimeter of fabric.

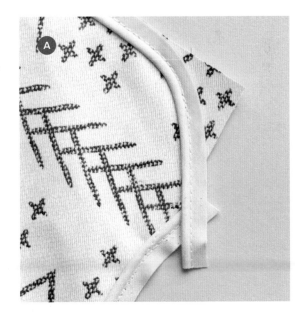

5   Place one of the back pieces face down on the front piece, line up
all three raw edges, and pin. Place the second back piece face down,
overlapping the first on the hemmed side, and line up all three raw
edges to the front fabric and pin (photo B).

6   Using a zipper foot so you can get very close to the cording, straight
stitch with a ¼-inch (6 mm) seam around the entire perimeter, making
sure to backstitch at each end. Trim the end bits of piping hanging
out and trim excess off corners. Turn right side out through the
overlap in back, press, and insert pillow form.

Featured fabrics: Mosaic Tile
Sandtone and Orinoco Jungle Line
by holli_zollinger, Vintage Moroccan –
Bone by littlearrowdesign, Adobo
Multi Sky by holli_zollinger

Tie-On Seat Cushion

Give the hard ladder chairs in your kitchen a comfy makeover with tie-on seat cushions.

MATERIALS + TOOLS

1 yard (91 cm) of woven fabric
16-inch (40.5 cm) square
    pillow insert
Basic sewing kit (see page 12)

1   Cut from the fabric one 31-inch (79 cm) by 16½-inch (42 cm) piece and one 7-inch (18 cm) by 16½-inch (42 cm) piece for the cushion body. Cut an additional four 13-inch (33 cm) by 1½-inch (4 cm) strips for the ties.

2   Press the long edges of the ties ¼ inch (6 mm) to the wrong side, and then fold each piece in half lengthwise and press. Topstitch along the folded, open side very near to the edge, making sure to backstitch at each end. Repeat for all four ties.

3   Lay the larger rectangle of fabric right side up. On one of the 16½-inch (42 cm) edges, measure 3 inches (7.5 cm) from each corner. To each point, pin one end of a tie so it lies perpendicular to the edge, with ½ inch (1.3 cm) extending over the raw edge, and then baste to hold in place (photo A).

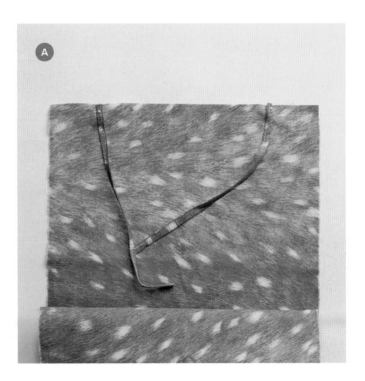

The following fabric was used for this project: Spoonflower's Linen Cotton Canvas in Soft Deer Hide by willowlanetextiles

4   Place the 7-inch (18 cm) by 16½-inch (42 cm) piece of fabric face down over the top of it, lining up the 16½-inch (42 cm) edges and pinning in place. Straight stitch this length with a ⅜-inch seam (1 cm), backstitching at each end. Trim the excess tie extending past the seam.

5   Hem the opposite 16½-inch (42 cm) side of the shorter rectangle. Fold to the wrong side ¼ inch (6 mm), and press, then fold again ½ inch (1.3 cm) and press and topstitch ⅜ inch (1 cm) from edge.

6   On the remaining 16½-inch (42 cm) side of the larger rectangle, fold to wrong side ¼ inch (6 mm) and press. Measure 3 inches (7.5 cm) from each corner and pin a tie as you did before. Baste to hold. Fold the edge ½ inch (1.3 cm) to the wrong side and press, then topstitch ⅜ inch (1 cm) from edge.

7   On the raw ends of all ties, fold twice, ¼ inch (6 mm), then ½ inch (1.3 cm) and topstitch back and forth a few times to close.

8   Lay your work right side up in front of you. Fold the larger piece in half so the ties line up with those on the opposite side. Fold the smaller piece at the seam over top of it (photo B). You should have a rough (not exact) square. Pin and then stitch with a ¼-inch (6 mm) seam around the entire perimeter.

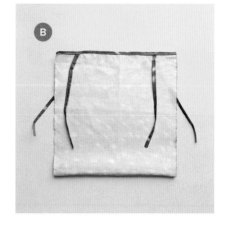

9   Trim excess off the corners and turn pillow cover right side out. Slide in the pillow insert to complete.

Knitting Caddy

Sew this vintage-inspired folding caddy with a yard of fabric and a few basic materials from the hardware store—it makes an adorable living room repository for your in-process knitting, half-read magazines, or errant toys.

MATERIALS + TOOLS

Four 15-inch (38 cm) lengths of ¾-inch (2 cm) wide flat wood moulding

Four 15-inch (38 cm) lengths of ½-inch (2 cm) round wood dowels

Linseed oil and rag for application

1 yard (91 cm) of lightweight cotton twill or linen cotton canvas fabric

3 yards (274 cm) of 1-inch (2.5 cm) bias binding

Basic sewing kit (see page 12)

Masking tape and a pen for labeling fabric components

Eight ¾-inch (2 cm) brass flat head wood screws

Two ½-inch (1.3 cm) screw posts

Drill

1 Take an old rag and rub the wooden components with a very tiny bit of linseed oil, then set aside to dry. You don't want wet, oily wood—use just enough to give the inexpensive wood a bit of luster.

2 Cut the fabric into the following pieces. Use masking tape and a pen to label if desired:

+ Two 12½-inch (32 cm) by 14-inch (35.5 cm) rectangles, labeled "front." If your print has a direction, cut so that the 12½-inch (32 cm) dimension is on the sides.

+ One 28-inch (71 cm) by 7-inch (18 cm) rectangle, labeled "middle."

+ Two 14-inch (35.5 cm) by 7-inch (18 cm) rectangles, each labeled "pocket." The 7-inch (18 cm) dimension is on the sides.

+ One 13-inch (33 cm) by 10½-inch (26.5 cm) rectangle, labeled "bottom."

3 At the top edge of a pocket piece, sew a 14-inch (35.5 cm) length of bias binding. Open up the binding, and pin it right side against the wrong side of the fabric, raw edges together. Straight stitch between the edge and the fold. Wrap around and refold along the raw edge of fabric, then topstitch. Repeat on second pocket piece.

4 Using the same method, sew 7-inch (18 cm) lengths of binding on the short sides of the middle piece.

5 Place a pocket piece right side up on top of a front piece (also right side up), lining the bottom edges together. Pin the sides, bottom edges, and top of pocket to front piece. Measure 4¾ inches (12 cm) from each side of the pocket and place a piece of masking tape from top to bottom as

The following fabric was used for this project: Spoonflower's Lightweight Cotton Twill in Watercolor Leaves by shopcabin

a guide. Backstitch, then topstitch from the binding to the bottom edge along these guides to create three pockets. Repeat these steps with second front piece.

6   Take the bottom piece and hem both 10½-inch (26.5 cm) sides: Fold and press to the wrong side ⅜ inch (1 cm), then fold again ⅜ inch (1 cm) and press. Topstitch.

7   Lay the middle piece flat in front of you, right side up. Place the bottom piece on top, right side up and centered. Line up raw edges on one side of the pieces and pin. Baste along this length (photo A).

8   Rotate the two pieces and line up the opposite raw edges. Pin and baste this length.

9   Center one of these basted sides to the bottom edge of one of the front pieces, wrong sides together. Pin along this length, then continue pinning raw edges of the middle piece up along both sides of the front piece. Baste very near the seam along the part you've pinned (photo B).

10 Open up bias binding and pin right side raw edge to the right side of the middle fabric. Sew bias binding from the top of one side of the front piece around the part you've basted together to enclose the seam, and then until you reach the top of the opposite side of the front piece. As you reach the corners, stop and remove work from machine to miter the corners by pressing them in place with your fingers. Refold binding around the seam and topstitch to secure, taking care on corners (photo C). Repeat with second front piece and opposite side of middle piece.

11 At the top of each front piece, fold the fabric over toward the wrong side ⅜ inch (1 cm) and press. Fold again 1½ inches (4 cm) and press. Topstitch 1¼ inches (3 cm) from edge to create a casing along the top, then repeat with opposite front piece. This completes the caddy—now let's put the wood supports together.

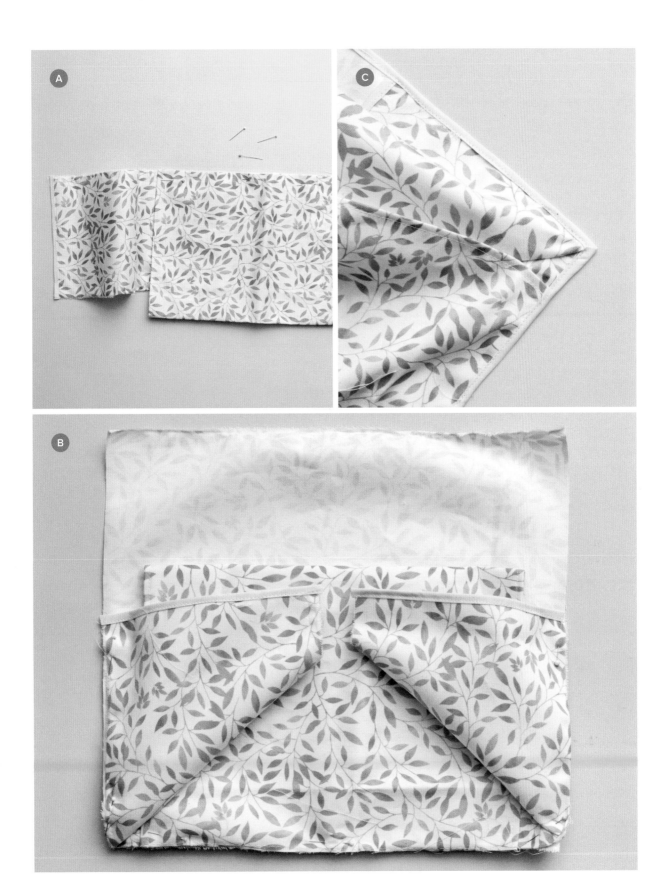

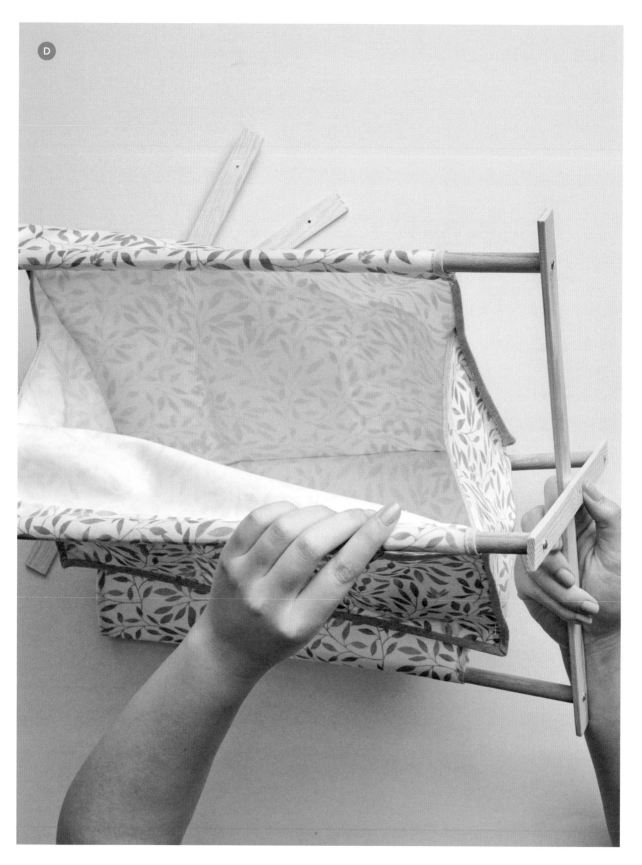

12 Mark each flat dowel with a pencil ¾ inch (2 cm) from one side and 1¼ inch (3 cm) from the opposite side. The ¾-inch (2 cm) sides are the "tops" of your flat dowels. Measure and mark the center 7½ inch (19 cm) of each dowel as well.

13 Predrill holes through all end marks, but not the center ones. Predrill a tiny ⅛ inch (3 mm) hole in the center of each end of the round dowels. Take one of the ¾-inch (2 cm) screws and screw through the top hole of one flat dowel into the end of one round dowel. Repeat with bottom hole and a second round dowel.

14 Take a second flat dowel and repeat steps, attaching two remaining round dowels to each end as above.

15 Arrange flat dowels together in an X and slide fabric onto dowels as shown (photo D).

16 Attach a flat dowel to the opposite ends of the round dowels by screwing into the holes you've predrilled.

    Note: Whichever flat dowel is farthest from fabric caddy on one side needs to be nearest fabric on this opposite side, so attach its second flat dowel first.

17 On one side, arrange the dowels in an X (they won't sit securely in place yet) so the middle marks on the flat dowels are aligned, then drill a ¼-inch (6 mm) or ⁵⁄₁₆-inch (8 mm) wide hole through both flat dowels. Insert one of the screw posts. Repeat on opposite side of caddy. And voilà! Your caddy will stand up on its own, but the bottom fabric piece gives it enough slack to allow it to fold. Isn't it beautiful?

Amy Steele of willowlanetextiles

Amy Steele taught herself early to embroider designs freehand on linen and was always engrossed in a sewing project as a child. Her Spoonflower shop, willowlanetextiles, now has a devout following for her designs of faux finishes, such as deer hides, gilded marble, abstracts, florals, quatrefoil and much more.

Part of her shop's appeal is in its approachability: willowlanetextiles welcomes requests for color revisions, coordinating looks for current designs, or something entirely new. "The aim is to help clients create an entire room of coordinating fabrics and papers effortlessly," said Steele.

Whether creating is a full-time outlet or a weekend hobby, Steele notes that it's important to find your vision. "My family inspires me more than anything," she said. "Just get started—inspiration will find you working!"

The Fabrics

These fabrics have an earthy, genuine look to them that will help bring nature into your home. Prints like Birch Grove are great for hiding seams as you line up the pattern, and Birch Bark can help hide mistakes when you need it. Deer Hide and Textured Mudcloth are great for the Tie-On Seat Cushion (page 113) and even the Drink Coasters (page 53).

We chatted with Amy from willowlanetextiles and here's some of what she had to say:

What's the first thing you do when you wake up?

"My day starts with a steaming cup of coffee, accompanied by a scratchpad and often a snuggly five-year-old on my lap. The numerous thoughts already swirling in my head make their way to paper, and a plan is made for the day. One of my most favorite activities is making lists!"

When did you first decide you wanted to create?

"I fell in love with design as a teenager. My dad bought me a sewing machine and I taught myself to embroider designs freehand on linen. I guess I was an odd kid . . . my favorite shops were fabric and craft stores, and I'd shut myself in my room for days, engrossed in a sewing project. I made my own clothes, coats, and even luggage!"

Featured willowlanetextiles fabrics, from left (top to bottom) to right (top to bottom): Deer Hide, Reclaimed Planks, Birch Grove, Carrera Marble Herringbone, Birch Bark; border design Carrera Marble

Alphabet Bunting

This is a simple method for creating a hanging message banner for your next party, a special day, or just to decorate a room. Since the letters are strung together by loops of ribbon, you can easily remove and reuse them, add more letters later, and customize your banner to your heart's content. And since you'll create the letter pattern at home using a printer, you can have lots of fun with different fonts (see Tip, next page) or changing the size of the letters as well.

MATERIALS + TOOLS

Basic sewing kit (see page 12)
Computer and printer
1 yard (91 cm) of lightweight cotton twill or linen cotton canvas
1 yard (91 cm) of interfacing
1 yard (91 cm) of quilt batting
Fabric chalk or pencil
1 yard (91 cm) of solid-colored ribbon (½ inch [1.3 cm] or ¼ inch [6 mm] wide)
Baker's twine

1   Using any word processing software, start a new file and type a single capital letter in a sans-serif, bold typeface (try Arial or Helvetica). Enlarge the letter until it fills the page and print. Cut out carefully and set aside— this will be your pattern. Repeat for all individual letters needed for banner.

2   With the fabric folded, cut two rectangles slightly larger than the first letter pattern and iron the interfacing onto the wrong side of both pieces. Cut a rectangle of batting roughly the same size at the two fabric pieces and sandwich between them (right sides of fabric facing outward). Pin the layers together with a few pins. Place the paper letter pattern on top of the fabric and trace around it with a pencil or fabric chalk.

3   Cut a 2-inch (5 cm) piece of ribbon and fold in half. Tuck ⅓ of its ends between the layers of fabric at the top center of the letter and pin in place (photo A). If the letter you're working on has two "tops" (such as an H, M, X or Y), add a ribbon loop to both.

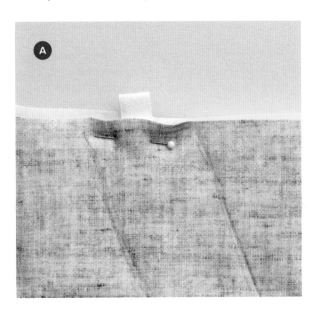

The following fabric was used for this project: Spoonflower's Linen Cotton Canvas in Solid Linen – Neutral by nouveau_bohemian

4 Straight stitch through all the layers, following the lines you've traced and making sure to sew through the ribbon ends as well.

5 Cut around the line you've stitched roughly ¼ inch from the stitches. When you reach the ribbon loops, cut one side of the fabric and then the other to avoid cutting the ribbon loop by accident (photo B).

6 Repeat steps for each letter. To finish, first lay out your letters on a flat surface, spaced evenly. Measure a length of baker's twine as long as this arrangement, and add another 2½ feet (76 cm). Cut. Thread the string through the ribbon of the first letter twice in a loop (this will keep it from sliding around), about 12 to 15 inches (30.5 to 38 cm) from the beginning of the string. Add the remaining letters in this same way down the line until your message is threaded and ready to hang!

Tip:

+ **Choosing a font for your letters:** We suggest bold and sans serif for this project because they are easy to cut and even easier to sew. Remember, you'll be sewing around them—a typeface with serifs, curlicues, and intricate flourishes can lead to major headaches at the sewing machine. However, with this in mind there is no reason to avoid fussy fonts entirely. After tracing the letter onto the fabric you could sew a simplified shape to connect the layers (skipping tiny details and sewing rather like it was a blobby version of itself), and then still cut it out following the original chalk pattern. Because the interfacing you add will actually keep the fabric from major fraying, and bunting is not really meant to be washed, the unfinished edges shouldn't be a problem.

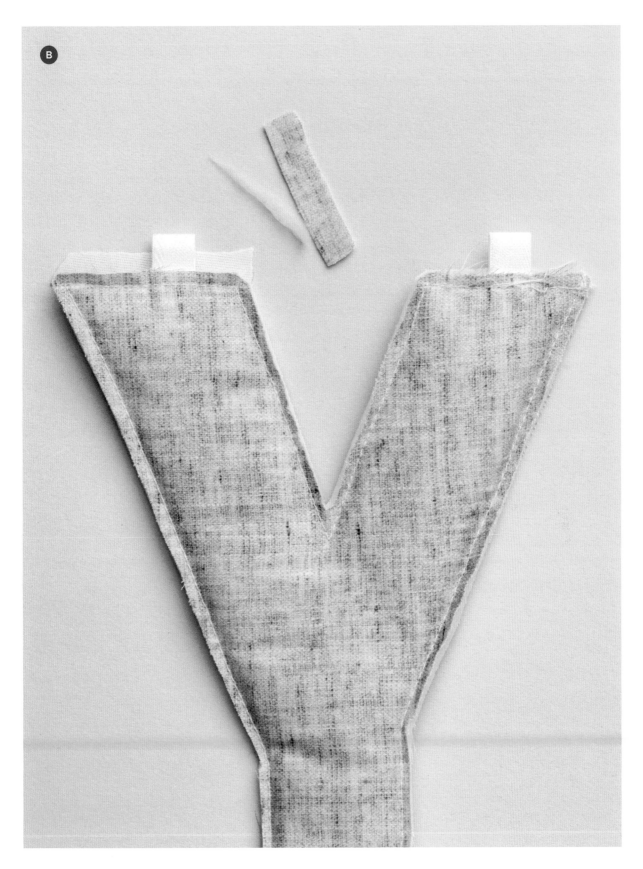

Advent Calendar

For this hanging advent calendar we wanted to try to get twenty-four pockets from one 36-inch (91 cm) by 42-inch (106 cm) yard of quilting-weight fabric. That equals cute but *tiny* little pockets, just right for a few pieces of candy or a little toy. We found this worked well if we wanted to use the pockets as stocking stuffer containers, ties to the outsides of gifts, or to tuck into the branches of the tree without them falling heavily to the floor. However, if you'd like larger pockets, just increase the square dimensions—all other steps remain the same.

MATERIALS + TOOLS

Scanner
Basic sewing kit (see page 12)
One 36-inch (91 cm) by 42-inch (106 cm) yard of quilting-weight fabric
8-inch (20 cm) square swatch of numbers (use template on page 180, or create your own)
1½ yards (366 cm) of ⅛-inch elastic cord (in a matching color)
24¾-inch (63 cm) self-cover button shanks, or make your own (see page 22)
A few yards of baker's twine, ribbon, or string to hang pockets as a garland

Featured fabrics, from top left to bottom: Snowflakes on Navy by caja_design, Little Trees Tan by mintpeony, Winter Dreams Nutcraker by shopcabin, Christmas Pine Trees by heleen_vd_thillart, Peppermint Candies by weavingmajor, Cal Tree Mint by scrummy, Fa La La La La by littlearrowdesign, Family Gatherings by papercanoefabricshop, Unknown, Retro Twinkle Lights by shelbyallison, Vintage Christmas Holiday by littlesmilemakers, and Stockings by misstiina

1   Scan the number button design (page 180) at 300 DPI and upload to Spoonflower, then order an 8-inch (20 cm) square test swatch. The grid image should exactly fill the swatch.

2   Using your rotary cutter, cutting surface, and a ruler, cut the yard of fabric into 96 4-inch (10 cm) squares. Each pocket will be made of four squares (two outer and two for the lining). If using multiple fabrics instead of one design for every pocket, divide the squares up now to keep everything organized.

3   Place a lining and an outer piece right sides together. Straight stitch a ¼-inch (6 mm) seam along one side of the fabric.

    Note: If the fabric has a direction, sew the top seam.

4   Repeat with the next two outer/lining squares, except this time cut a 2-inch (5 cm) length of elastic cord and fold in half. Tie the end in a knot to make it easier to work with, then tuck the cord folded-end first between the seam, and pin in place (photo A). Then, straight stitch the seam as before, sewing over the cord to make a little loop (this will be to fasten the shank button).

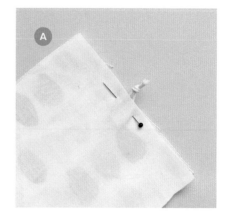

5   Open up your sewn pieces and press the seams open. Place the right sides together (lining against lining and outer against outer), and pin. Straight stitch a ¼-inch (6 mm) seam along both long sides and along the bottom of the outer fabric.

6   Trim off the excess at corners and turn right side out. Sew a straight stitch ⅜-inch (1 cm) from raw edge to close the remaining open lining seam, then tuck the lining into the outer part so that you have a 3½-inch (9 cm) square pocket. Press flat. Repeat these steps until you have 24 pockets.

7   Cut out all the button numbers (follow the circle guides). If you have self-covering buttons, place a circle face down and centered into the button mold, and place a front piece face down after it. The fabric will naturally bunch and fold over top of the back of the button piece (photo B). Tuck it in completely and then place the back button part over the bunched-up fabric, shank out. Use the hard plastic tool provided to press the back part into the front, sealing up the fabric around the button. Repeat with remaining 23 buttons.

8   On each pocket, make a little pencil mark 2 inches (5 cm) from the top center on the opposite side of the pocket from the elastic loop. Attach the buttons here.

9   Fill all the pockets with candy or small treasures like stickers, erasers, temporary tattoos, etc. To finish, just fold the top of the pocket with the loop over the baker's twine and fasten around the button. Repeat with pocket after pocket, all along your length of twine until you have a garland of them.

Tip:

+   If you don't have or want to use covered number buttons, there are many creative ways to number your advent calendar instead. Hand embroidery, paper tags tied around the buttons with baker's twine, or fabric appliqués are just a few methods for numbering. Keep in mind you'll need numbers 1–24!

Dress-Up Clothes

Dress-up clothing is irresistible and every house should have a full-to-bursting costume trunk. (Kids to enjoy it are optional.) Dress-up clothing can save the day when you find yourself desperately needing a last-minute costume for a party or are looking for a way to keep the kids away from the television on a rainy day. These four very basic costume ideas can be sewn from solid fabric, or a lovely print. (And will look even better if you make several of each.)

MATERIALS + TOOLS

1 yard (91 cm) of fleece or other knit fabric

Plate with a 7-inch (18 cm) diameter

Thumbtack

1 yard (91 cm) of string

A pencil or washable pen

Basic sewing kit (see page 12)

The following fabrics were used for these projects: (Wings) Spoonflower's Organic Cotton Knit in Island Blue Diamonds by laurapol; (Crown) Spoonflower's Cotton Poplin in Solid Linen – Neutral by nouveau_bohemian; (Rabbit Hat) Spoonflower's Cotton Poplin in Watercolor Floral Red by laurapol

Nearly Instant Wings

This costume requires just a tiny bit of measuring, a little fussy tracing, a small amount of cutting, and then just two straight stitches. That's it. Since we're using knit fabric, the edges will roll and there isn't any need to hem or finish them. You can have a lot of fun designing your own fabric for this—check the sidebar for tips on how to get your kids involved in fabric design, too.

1   Have your bird extend their arms straight out, and measure their wingspan from wrist to wrist. For this project I'm going to use 36 inches (91 cm) as an example.

2   Cut the fabric into a rectangle that is 36 inches (91 cm) by 28 inches (71 cm). The 28-inch (71 cm) side can also be adjusted for a taller or littler bird. If the fabric isn't four-way stretch, cut it so that it stretches along the 28-inch (71 cm) side.

3   Fold the top of the rectangle over 4½ inches (11.5 cm) where the fabric will lie across the shoulders to the wrong side and pin. Fold the fabric in half to the 28-inch (71 cm) side, with right sides together.

4   Place the plate in the top folded corner and trace around it to make a quarter circle and cut out. Trim off the folded fabric straight down as shown (photo A).

5   Use the plate to trace half-circles along an arc from bottom corner and fold up to the opposite raw edge to make scallops. Cut along this scalloped edge (photo B).

6 Unfold the fabric so it is a scalloped half-circle, but leave the 4½-inch (11.5 cm) side pinned. Topstitch the pinned edges with a zigzag stitch, making sure to backstitch at each end. These are now the armholes, and your bird is ready to fly.

Tip:

+ **Rainy Day Activity:** Have your kids and their friends create the fabric for these dress-up projects. Fill up letter-sized white paper with drawings of diamonds and gemstones for the crown. Draw a page of dashes, dots, scribbly lines, or zigzags for the rabbit ears. A wonderful bird-wing print can be made by drawing Vs horizontally across the paper for feathers and coloring. Don't be afraid to mix media: markers, crayons, cut or ripped paper, and colored pencils all together look so great when printed! Scan everything at 300 DPI and upload to Spoonflower—you can reduce the size of the print before ordering if it seems too large.

MATERIALS + TOOLS

Two 24-inch (61 cm) by 6-inch
  (15 cm) pieces of Kona®
  Cotton or cotton poplin
  fabric
Wrapping paper or recycled
  paper bag to draw a pattern
Two 24-inch (61 cm) by
  6-inch (15 cm) pieces of
  heavyweight interfacing
24-inch (61 cm) length of 1-inch
  (2.5 cm) double-fold bias
  binding
2 inches (5 cm) of 1-inch
  (2.5 cm) Velcro, or two snaps
  and tool
Basic sewing kit (see page 12)

Crown

These are so quick to make, you can sew a dozen for a birthday party or school play easily. Have fun with the shape of the crown, but keep in mind you'll be outlining it with a straight stitch and turning—so keep the design a solid form without holes.

1   If possible, measure your royal's head circumference. Add 1½ inch (4 cm) to this measurement. If you don't have a head around to measure, a toddler's average head is 16 inches (40.5 cm), a child's head is 18 inches (46 cm), and an adult's head is 21 inches (53 cm) to 23 inches (58 cm).

2   Draw a basic crown shape (perhaps a long rectangle with pointy triangles along the top) in the length you've measured, on the back of some wrapping paper or an unfolded paper grocery bag.

3   Trace the shape onto the back of your fabric with a fabric pen and then add a ⅜-inch (1 cm) seam allowance.

4   Cut two pieces of fabric from this pattern, for both the outside and inside of the crown. Cut two pieces of heavy weight interfacing from the pattern without the seam allowance, then iron the interfacing onto the wrong side of the fabric.

5   With the right sides facing in, sew a straight stitch ⅜ inch (1 cm) from the edge of the sides and top points of the crown. Leave the bottom edge open.

6   Notch the top of the crown's points and in between each point as well. Turn right side out and press. If you've used two different fabrics for the crown, decide which one is the outside.

7   Unfold the bias binding. At one end, tuck about ¾ inch (2 cm) of the bias tape under itself and pin along the bottom raw edge of inner fabric, right sides together (photo A). At opposite end, tuck another ¾ inch (2 cm) of binding under itself. Straight stitch the bias tape along the bottom edge of the crown. Wrap bias binding around raw edge and refold. Topstitch binding (photo B).

8 At this point, we like to check the fit again on the intended king or queen's head before closing it up. To finish, sew Velcro on each side of crown ¼ inch (6 mm) from sides. Cut about 2 inches (5 cm) of Velcro and sew one half of it to the inner fabric on one end of crown, and the opposite half to the outer fabric on opposite side. If you're a snap tool addict like me, you can close with snaps instead (I love Dritz Color Snaps)—mark where the crown ends should layer for the best fit as a guide.

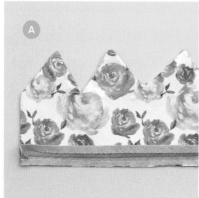

MATERIALS + TOOLS
Scanner and printer
1 yard (91 cm) cotton knit
12-inch (30.5 cm) by 8-inch (20 cm) fleece or minky fabric for inside of ears
Basic sewing kit (see page 12)
Optional: serger (will make sewing knits a breeze and eliminates bulk when using fleece)

Rabbit Hat

1 Enlarge the child-sized bike cap pattern on page 176 and print (you'll just need the crown). Enlarge the rabbit hat brim and ear pattern on page 181 and print.

2 Trace the pattern pieces onto the fabric and cut out. On the fleece ear pieces, mark the fabric where indicated on the pattern by the dots. Fold each crown piece in half (right side of fabric inward) so that the points align, and pin. Stitch with a ¼-inch (6 mm) seam from fold to top of point. Repeat for all eight crown pieces. Notch the fabric on these curved seams.

3 Pin two of the outer crown pieces with right sides together along one curve, with points aligning. Stitch a ¼-inch (6 mm) seam. Repeat with the next two outer crown pieces. Notch the curved seams, and press open.

4   With right sides of fabric together (one piece of your main fabric and one from your fleece), stitch around perimeter of each ear piece, leaving the bottom (the side marked with dots) open for turning. Turn right side out and press.

5   Fold the fleece side of the ears until the points you've marked line up. Pin these folded ends to the right side of one half of the hat crown, 2½ inches (6.5 cm) from top center on each side (photo A). Place the other crown half on top, line up raw edges and pinch. Stitch with a ¼-inch (6 mm) seam. Notch curves and turn right side out.

6   Repeat these steps for the crown pieces of lining, except omit the part with the ears.

7   Line up edge C of the brim pieces with right sides together and sew with a ⅜-inch (1 cm) seam (photo B). Notch all curves. Line up D edges, right side together, and sew with a ⅜-inch (1 cm) seam (photo C). Turn right side out and press.

8   Place the lining inside the outer crown of the hat and line up the open edge at the bottom, right sides of both fabrics facing out. Pin the open edge of the brim piece around the outside of the crown, outer side against outer side with the brim's back seam at the center back of the crown (ears should be on either side). Sew a ½-inch (1.3 cm) seam with a serger or a zigzag stitch (photo D).

6

MULTI-YARD PROJECTS

Larger projects can seem daunting, with yards of fabric and loads of straight edges. However, we have found a few tips that help to ease our worries whenever we embark on a bigger sewing project. Just remember: Wash it, dry it, check the grain, iron it, and then begin your layout.

A few other tools that make the load lighter are using a washable pen, tailor's chalk, and a t-square to draw lines liberally on your fabric. We also use masking tape for marking lines, too, since it is easy to follow when sewing (we also "pin" with tape all the time). When making something really enormous, try rolling up the fabric you're not sewing so it doesn't hang heavily off the table and pull the piece out of shape. Or, if you have an extra table, push it up against your sewing table to extend your work surface.

We promise, there is no reason to be intimidated by huge swaths of fabric. By the end of this section you'll have made a picnic blanket (page 147), hanging doorway puppet theater (page 161) and an entire chair (page 153) and you'll wonder why you ever worried in the first place. So, choose a fabric you've had your eye on, order three yards, and let's go.

Featured fabric:
Flying South by nouveau_bohemian

Play Tent

This is a simple tent with deceptively easy construction. It folds flat, so it can be transported to the beach or park (or stored when *not* needed), but is still delightfully inviting just hanging out in a playroom or reading corner of the classroom. Place it on top of the picnic blanket (page 147) and toss some pillows inside (page 109) to complete the coziness factor. This one is fun to experiment with different fabrics—a more sheer fabric will let light through an indoor tent, while heavy Eco Canvas will be easy to wipe clean and more durable if you're toting it around.

MATERIALS + TOOLS

Basic sewing kit (see page 12)
3 yards (274 m) of linen cotton canvas or twill fabric
One ½-inch (1.3 cm) by 42-inch round wood dowel
Four ⁷⁄₁₆-inch (1.1 cm) by 1⅝-inch (1.5 cm) by 48-inch lengths of flat wood moulding
Two ¼-inch (6 mm) by 1½-inch (4 cm) by 40-inch lengths of flat wood moulding
Drill with ½-inch (1.3 cm) bit
Four 1-inch (2.5 cm) flat head wood screws
Four clamps
Wood glue (optional)
4 feet of twine or cord

1   Cut the fabric to a 39-inch (99 cm) by 96-inch rectangle (244 cm).

2   Hem the long ends of the fabric by folding the fabric to the wrong side ½ inch (1.3 cm) twice, pressing and topstitching.

3   Fold the short ends of the fabric to the wrong side ½ inch (1.3 cm), and then fold again 2 inches (5 cm). Topstitch 1¾ inch (4.5 cm) from the edge to create casings.

4   On all four lengths of the 1⅝-inch moulding, measure and mark 1½ inch (4 cm) from one end. Drill a centered ½-inch (1.3 cm) hole in each piece where you've marked.

5   Slide a dowel through the holes you've drilled, and arrange your tent structure like the diagram shown below, with two flat moulding pieces at each side and 1 inch (2.5 cm) of the dowel extending from each end.

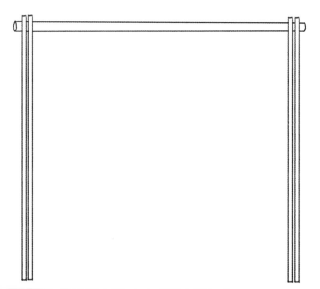

The following fabric was used for this project: Spoonflower's Lightweight Cotton Twill in Love, Carved in Birch by willowlanetextiles

6   Slide the shorter flat wood pieces through your casings at each end of the fabric. Clamp the ends to the bottom of moulding on one side of your tent, bring the fabric over the round dowel, and clamp the opposite wood piece to the bottom of the opposite side of tent. Adjust until the fabric is taut.

7   Attach the wood piece to tent bottoms with screws, and remove clamps (photo A).

8   Once the tent is open, use the twine or cord and tie to each side at the back. This keeps the tent from continuing to slide open and collapse. If you're placing the tent on carpeting you may not need this.

Tip:

+ If you don't own a drill (or ½-inch [1.3 cm] drill bit), see if the hardware store can drill the ½-inch (1.3 cm) holes for you, and use wood glue instead of screws to hold the bottom in place. Just be sure to keep everything clamped for twenty-four hours if so to be sure that it sets.

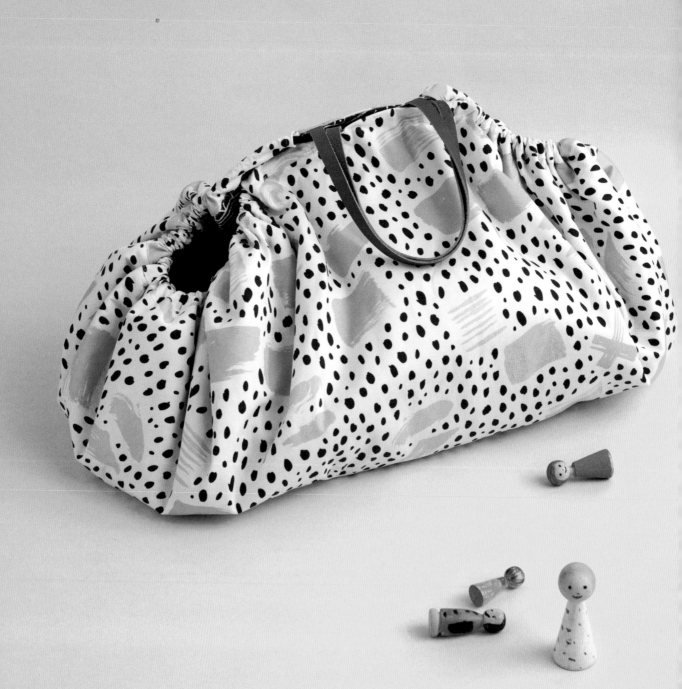

Drawstring Picnic Blanket

This circular blanket is sewn with a casing around the outside that can be cinched up when the picnic's over and used as a carry-all. We used Spoonflower's Eco Canvas for ours because it's easy to wipe clean and not as absorptive as cotton, and if you're taking yours outside more than in, you may consider this as well. However, this blanket is perfect as a playroom rug for instantaneous toy cleanup, in which case you could opt for a more plush fabric and can omit the carrying handles.

MATERIALS + TOOLS

2 yards (1.8 m) of eco canvas

2 yards (1.8 m) of eco canvas in a second print

48-inch square of 2 mm quilt batting

1 yard (91 cm) by ¾ inch (2 cm) wide flat leather or imitation leather strip

Ruler

Pencil

14 feet of ⅜-inch (1 cm) cotton rope

Large safety pin

Masking tape

Embroidery floss and embroidery needle

Basic sewing kit (see page 12) including a leather or denim needle

The following fabrics were used for this project: Spoonflower's Lightweight Cotton Twill in Strokes Dots Cross and Spots by littlesmilemakers and Chalk Tribal Stripe by leanne

1   Cut the fabric into two 48-inch squares—set aside the excess of the second print to make a wide bias strip later. Fold the first yard of fabric in half, then in half again. Iron it nice and flat. Measure and mark 24 inches (61 cm) from the folded corner in 2- to 3-inch (5-7.5 cm) increments along an arch, until you reach the opposite side. Connect the marks, pin, and cut along the arch, so when you unfold the fabric you have a circle. Use that circle as a pattern to cut out a matching circle of the second print and the quilt batting.

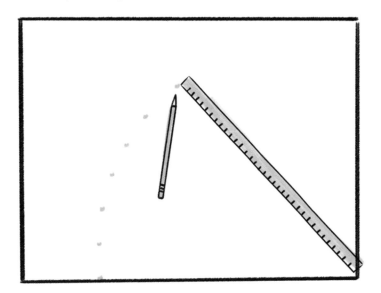

2   Cut the excess of your second print along the bias in 3-inch (7.5 cm) strips and sew the ends together until you have a long, continuous, 3-inch (7.5 cm) wide strip of fabric. Follow the instructions on page 16 to make your handmade bias tape; you'll need about 12 feet (3.7 m). Cut the strip into two lengths of 70 inches (178 cm).

3 Hem the short ends of the long strips by folding the fabric over ⅜ inch (1 cm) and pressing, then folding again ½ inch (1.3 cm). Press and topstitch. On both strips, with right side of fabric facing down, fold the fabric ¼ inch (6 mm) over along one long edge and press.

4 Take one of the large fabric circles and, with right sides together, pin the raw edges of one strip around the perimeter (photo A). Repeat with the second fabric strip, leaving 6-inch (15 cm) gaps between them on opposite sides of the circle. (If you end up with gaps that aren't 6 inches [15 cm], just adjust and re-pin so that both gaps are equal lengths and directly opposite each other on the circle.) Sew with a ⅜-inch (1 cm) seam along these edges.

5 Cut the leather strip into two 18-inch (46 cm) pieces. Take the first one and pin each end to the raw edge ½ inch (1.3 cm) from each side of one of the gaps, with the strap lying in an arc overtop the fabric. Baste ends in place, then repeat with second strap on opposite gap. I like to use a bit of masking tape to tape the straps to the fabric so they don't move around and get in the way until I'm done.

6 Place the second large fabric circle on top of the first with right sides together. Backstitch, and sew the two pieces together where the 5½ inch (14 cm) gaps are, with a ⅜-inch (1 cm) seam. Use a leather needle in your machine and go over the seam a second time for durability. Flip right side out, remove tape from straps to free them, and slide the quilt batting in between the two large fabric circles. Arrange and smooth with your hands until all the raw edges are aligned; make sure the casing fabric strip is entirely outside the circle as well.

7   Fold the casing fabric over about 1½ inches (4 cm) so the ¼-inch (6 mm) folded edge is lined up with the raw edge of the second fabric circle. This will create two 1½-inch (4 cm) tubes (casings) of fabric, each 51 inches long, around the circle. Pin like crazy and carefully press—don't try to skip pinning here unless you want a wonky mess.

8   Topstitch the casing (photo B). I like to use a looser zigzag stitch here to connect the circle to the folded edge of the casing.

9   Stick the safety pin through one end of the cotton rope, and use it to work the rope through the casing all the way around the circle. Knot the ends together.

10 To finish, we're going to quilt it a bit with ties. Take the masking tape and tape across one side of your blanket in straight lines about 3 inches (7.5 cm) apart. Tape across perpendicular to these lines, also 3 inches (7.5 cm) apart, so you have a grid. Hand sew through one side of the blanket and back out again in the center of each square with the embroidery floss. Don't knot the end of the floss, just leave a 2-inch (5 cm) tail on each side of the stitch, then trim and tie in a double knot. Repeat for all the squares, and remove the tape (photo C).

You can pull the blanket closed with the rope and then carry it like a shoulder bag using the leather straps. Now all that's left are beach towels, a thermos of something refreshing, and a good book.

Esther Fallon Lau of nouveau_bohemian

There's a childlike wonder that occurs whenever someone discovers Esther Fallon Lau's shop, nouveau_bohemian, for the first time. The rich watercolors and fantastical creatures evoke undiscovered worlds—tapping into the dreamers within us all.

Lau wasn't always creative professionally, holding a string of "serious" jobs, from working in the prime minister's department to working on big government initiatives to grow industry. Eventually, she felt she had missed her calling and turned back to her roots, discovering Spoonflower along the way.

Lau's vibrant life now takes place in a rainforest-like valley in the foothills around the world-famous coastal town of Byron Bay, Australia, which inspires her designs. "Mother Nature is the High Queen of Design," she said. "I have always been an avid collector and arranger of shells, seed pods, flowers, and feathers."

The Fabrics

Nouveau_bohemian has a great selection of geometric and scenic patterns, perfect for both large and small projects. When working with fabrics like Good Shot (Mustard), be sure to align the straight edges at the end of the pattern for a clean look. For fabrics with scenes, such as Max's Map (Grey) and Arctic Song, try to use the full scene: cut sections of fabric to include the most detail so that the scenes stay recognizable. Nouveau_bohemian's fabrics also offer a lot of fun potential—try mixing a geometric pattern like Hexo (Blue) with something more playful like Markings (Raw Linen). You might be pleasantly surprised by the outcome!

Talking with Esther from nouveau_bohemian about the details of her day and her work:

How does your average day begin?

"Inhumanely early with my baby yelling at me; then cuddles in the 'cuddle chair' with my two bigger boys and an endless round of herding, feeding, and preventing these three wild animals from dying (in the dam, flooded creeks, tree houses, explorations in the bush, bike jumps, etc.) and overseeing their elaborate creative 'projects.' Designing happens in the cracks, mostly in my mind. I compose layouts, add texture, flip through palette options all inside my brain while I am sweeping, driving, falling asleep. The best thing about this is that it keeps the ideas fluid, so I can chase the 'feeling' of a design right down the rabbit hole without choking it too soon. The physical act of designing is crammed into the two tiny windows when my baby is asleep each day . . . so in these moments I am a ferociously-focused, uber-efficient powerhouse."

I'd love to see one of my designs turned into:

"A theme park."

My favorite Spoonflower fabric to work with is:

"Minky. I sew lots of throw cushions for my kids' schools and friends' children. Kids love that fabric. My son says it feels like he is snuggling a polar bear."

Featured nouveau_bohemian fabrics, from top to bottom:
Max's Map (Grey), Narwhal Symphony (Aqua), Markings (Raw Linen),
Hexo (Blue); border design Solitude (Earth)

Pyramid Beanbag Chair

We're not exactly sure when we realized that sewing giant pillows and cushions was exactly like sewing little pillows and cushions, just with lots more fabric and thread. But when we did, it was an amazing revelation, because here was a way to not just decorate around the house with fabric we love, but create actual furniture with fabric we love.

Remember when we made beanbags a few sections back? Well, this project is just like that, except now we'll add a zipper using the easiest installation method in the history of zippers. And if you're thinking that beanbags are for preschools and '80s rec rooms, consider giving this chair some class by using a luxe home décor fabric like velvet.

MATERIALS + TOOLS

2 yards (1.8 m) of medium to heavyweight woven fabric
24-inch (61 cm) zipper
6 cubic feet (170 L) of beanbag filling
Beanbag net liner
Basic sewing kit (see page 12)
Zipper foot
8-inch (20 cm) diameter plate

The following fabric was used for this project: Spoonflower's Celosia Velvet™ in Monstera Leaves by crystal_walen

1   Cut the fabric into two 36-inch (91 cm) by 42-inch rectangles and pin right sides together.

2   Sew the two long edges with a ½-inch (1.3 mm) seam in a short stitch. You may want to sew a double seam for durability.

3   Open the tube on one side and refold (still right sides together) to align the two opposite seams so they meet in the center, and pin (photo A). Put your zipper down against this edge and mark on the fabric where the metal stops are at each end. Remove the zipper, and straight stitch a ¾-inch (2 cm) seam

with a very short stitch from the corners to each point you've marked. Backstitch at each end. Then, using the longest stitch your machine has, baste without backstitching the remaining opening.

4   Open up the project as best you can so this seam lies flat (the tube will be all bunched up) and press open. Place the zipper face down along the basted part of the seam and pin. Using a zipper foot, sew with a straight stitch on either side of the zipper, backstitching at each end. When you

Tip:

+ Filling your beanbag chair: Commercially available expanded polystyrene (EPS) beads are what fills most beanbag chairs in the US. The tiny plastic beads are not biodegradable, but can be recycled at appropriate locations and reused at home for craft projects or as soil filler in house plants once the lifespan of your chair eventually wears out. Those searching for a natural alternative to EPS are often choosing buckwheat hulls as filler. They are a bit harder than Styrofoam beads, but are a much more earth-friendly option. Search online and you'll find them available everywhere.

reach where the zipper head is, lower the foot and carefully open the zipper past the foot to get it out of the way, and then finish sewing. Use a seam ripper to open the basted seam and then open the zipper.

5   Refold the fabric so the two pieces of main fabric are lying right side together again with the seams on the sides, and then fold in half lengthwise so that the corners meet. Trace around the plate to round these corners (photo B). Unfold fabric.

6   Line up the remaining raw edge. Sew a ⅜-inch (1 cm) seam with a short stitch. You can go over this seam twice for durability.

7   Turn right side out, fill the beanbag liner with the filling, and then ease it into the beanbag and zip closed.

Plush Bear Rug

This fuzzy faux bear rug is tied with the pet bandanas for the cutest project in this book, as well as the most animal-friendly. Accentuate its cruelty-free fakeness by choosing a bright, abstract print for the minky fur. If you're searching for something that coordinates with a room, designing your own bear fabric is easy. Simply cover a page of colored construction paper with hand-drawn Vs or Is (use a white paint marker or gel pen on dark paper), scan to Spoonflower at 300 DPI, and adjust the size of the marks in preview before ordering.

MATERIALS + TOOLS

Scanner and printer

Basic sewing kit (see page 12)

1 yard (91 cm) plus 1 fat quarter of minky fabric for top of rug

1 yard (91 cm) of eco canvas for the bottom

Wrapping paper for drawing a large pattern

Swatch of black felt

Two 1-inch (91 cm) black buttons

Black embroidery floss and embroidery needle

Poly-fil stuffing for the head—a 12-oz. (55 g) bag is more than enough

1   Scan and enlarge the pattern pieces on page 182. Print and cut out the pieces.

2   Cut out the head pattern pieces from the fat quarter of fabric. Cut the nose from black felt. Notch or mark the fabric with a washable pen where noted on the pattern.

3   With right sides together, line up and sew the top of the nose to the bottom of the middle head piece with a ⅜-inch (1 cm) seam.

4   With right sides together, line up and pin one of the side head pieces to one side of the middle piece to the bottom tip of the nose (photo A). Sew with a ⅜-inch (1 cm) seam. Repeat with the opposite side of the head.

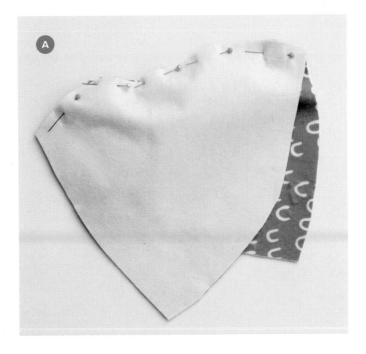

The following fabric was used for this project: Spoonflower's Minky in Scandinavian Lucky Horseshoe by littlesmilemakers

Tip:

+ Make this rug into a blanket by replacing the bottom fabric with a soft, lightweight cotton or organic knit, instead of the sturdier canvas we've used here. Just remember, it's extra important to prewash your fabric *before cutting* when pairing different fiber contents to avoid wonky shrinkage woes later.

5 Place two ear pieces right sides together and sew around the curve, leaving the bottom open. Notch the curve and turn, then repeat to make the second ear. Fold the front part of the ears so the fabric overlaps and baste to hold in place. Pin both to the areas on the head marked with EAR on the pattern, lining up the raw edges.

6 With right sides together, sew a ⅜-inch (1 cm) seam from the bottom of the nose to the back of the head to attach the two side head pieces together under the chin.

7 With right sides together, pin the back of the head piece around the back of the bear's head, lining up the dots. Sew with a ⅜-inch (1 cm) seam from dot to dot. Notch curves and turn right side out through the opening.

8 Sew the buttons onto the head with black embroidery floss. Use the embroidery floss to hand sew a smiling mouth if you wish. Tie off thread inside head. Stuff with Poly-fil and baste the opening of head closed.

9 Cut a piece of wrapping paper to 18-inch (46 cm) by 27-inch (69 cm). Lay it in front of you with the 18-inch (46 cm) dimension on the sides.

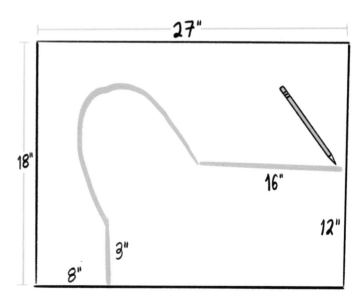

Mark 12 inches (30.5 cm) from the lower right corner up along right side, and draw a 16-inch line parallel to the lower edge. Mark 8 inches (20 cm) from the lower left corner along the lower edge, and draw a 3-inch (7.5 cm) line parallel to the left side. Now draw a curvy line as similar as you can to this diagram (opposite page).

10 Cut out this shape. This is your pattern for the body. Label the lower and right edges "fold."

11 Trim the minky and canvas fabric to 36 inch (91 cm) by 54 inch (137 cm). Fold one of the fabric pieces in half to the 54-inch (137 cm) sides, then fold in half again to the 36-inch (91 cm) sides. Arrange in front of you with the twice-folded corner at the lower right. Place the pattern on top of this rectangle, lining up the lower right corners, and cut out. Repeat with the second fabric.

12 Unfold and lay the two pieces right sides together, lining up and pinning the entire perimeter. Sew with a ⅜-inch (1 cm) seam, making sure to backstitch at each end, and leaving a 3½-inch (9 cm) opening in the center of one of the 6-inch (15 cm) edges. Think of this opening as the neck of the bear. Notch all curves and turn the fabric through this opening.

13 Place the basted part of the head into the opening and pin in place. Hand stitch the entire opening closed with an invisible stitch (photo B).

Doorway Puppet Theater

Before having kids, you may have imagined that you would be the sort of parent that created charming handmade playthings while crafting with your children in the kitchen in adorably mismatched smocks, all from your clean, spacious flat with pristine white walls and wooden floors.

However, if you're anything like us, this is absolutely not what happened, and every day is a daily challenge to pry the iPads out of their little hands. So, if you're looking at this project thinking *yeah, right*—we get it. However, if you can find an afternoon to sew it, you are sure to capture the imaginations of the kids in your life and provide an amazing amount of screen-free entertainment.

MATERIALS + TOOLS

Basic sewing kit (see page 12)

1 yard (91 cm) each of two designs of basic cotton fabric

1 yard (91 cm) of basic cotton or cotton poplin for stage curtain

One 28- to 40-inch (71 to 101 cm) tension shower curtain rod

Two ⅜-inch (1 cm) diameter dowels, cut to the width of your doorway

1   Measure the width of your doorway. Mine is 32 inches (81 cm), so that is the width I'll be using throughout this project, but if your doorway is wider or more narrow, just replace that measurement with your own.

2   Cut a 36-inch (91 cm) by 32-inch (81 cm) rectangle of cotton fabric for the lower half of the theater. Cut one 20-inch (51 cm) by 32-inch (81 cm) piece and two 7-inch (18 cm) by 16-inch (40.5 cm) pieces for the top half. Cut two 12-inch (30.5 cm) by 14-inch (35.5 cm) pieces and eight 2½-inch (6.5 cm) by 4½-inch (11.5 cm) strips of the cotton fabric. Finally, cut two 5-inch (14 cm) by 1½-inch (4 cm) strips and one 30-inch (76 cm) by 1½-inch (4 cm) strip of cotton fabric for casings for the dowel. These will be on the back of the theater and not visible, so they can be from scrap fabric if you like.

3   Hem the inner 16-inch (40.5 cm) sides of the 7-inch (18 cm) by 16-inch (40.5 cm) pieces ½ inch (1.3 cm) by pressing to wrong side ¼ inch (6 mm) twice, and topstitching with a straight stitch. Flip them over and pin the 5-inch (14 cm) by ½-inch (1.3 cm) strips straight across the top back edge, starting from the hem. These won't be visible on the front of the finished theater, so you can even use scrap fabric for this.

4   On both pieces, turn fabric back to right side and baste ¼ inch (6 mm) from top edge. Then topstitch securely 1 inch (2.5 cm) from top edge. This creates two quickie casings that will hold the stage curtain dowel later.

5   Press the bottom of the large top piece a ½ inch (1.3 cm) to the wrong side. With all fabric right side up, pin one of the basted side panels underneath

The following fabrics were used for this project: Spoonflower's Basic Cotton in Flying South and Birch Bears (Blue) and Solid Linen – Neutral by nouveau_bohemian

the folded bottom of this piece about ½ inch (1.3 cm) (photo A). Pin the second side panel on the opposite side of the top piece in the same way. Topstitch ¼ inch (6 mm) all the way across the bottom edge of this upper rectangle to attach the two side panels. If you have a double needle, you can use it here for extra durability, or you could also topstitch a second row above the first.

6   With right sides together, center the 30-inch (76 cm) by 1½-inch (4 cm) strip of fabric to the upper edge of the bottom fabric piece and sew with a ¼-inch (6 mm) seam (photo B). Press the strip of fabric to the wrong side of bottom fabric. Turn over and topstitch 1 inch (2.5 cm) from seam to create second casing.

7   Pin the lower fabric piece to the bottom edges of the side panels (right sides together) (photo C). Stitch a ¼-inch (6 mm) seam, backstitching at each end.

8   Your theater is starting to come together! You'll now have a nearly doorway-sized rectangle with a "stage" opening in the center of it. Press the entire perimeter ¼ inch (6 mm) to the wrong side twice, then topstitch to hem the whole thing. Be careful not to accidentally seal up the casings as you hem past them. (Note: if your theater seems too "tall" for your kids, just take some inches off the bottom edge and hem.)

9   At the top of the theater, fold over 2 inches (5 cm) to wrong side and press, then topstitch 1¾ inches (4.5 cm) to create a casing for the tension rod.

10 Hem the 14-inch (35.5 cm) edges of the curtain pieces by pressing ¼-inch (6 mm) to the wrong side twice and topstitching.

11 Press the long edges of all eight smaller pieces ¼ inch (6 mm) to the wrong sides and topstitch. Fold in half (lining up raw edges) and press. Pin four of these (raw edges aligned) evenly across the top raw edge of one of the curtain pieces and sew with a ½-inch (1.3 cm) seam. Press seam to wrong side of curtain, turn over, and topstitch. Hem the bottom edge by pressing ¼ inch (6 mm) twice and topstitching. Repeat with second curtain piece.

12 Slide a dowel through one side of the casing at the top of theater window, thread the two curtains onto it, then slide through casing on the opposite side. Slide a dowel through the lower casing (photo D). This second dowel is not as crucial at the first, but serves to stabilize the theater and keep it from sagging. Slide the tension rod through the casing at the top of your theater and hang.

Tip:

+ This theater is beautiful and simple as is, but is also really fun to embellish. Iron fusible interfacing to the back of contrasting fabric, print and cut out paper letters, then use them as a pattern to cut fabric appliqués and iron onto the front to make a sign. Or make tassels from your jersey knit yarn (see page 29) and hang across the top in a garland. Your craft store should have an inspiring array of trims meant for curtains: fringe, beads, and ribbon trims can all be used to make your theater special.

Featured fabrics: Falling Triangle – Dusty Blue by littlearrowdesign, Birch Bears (Blue) by nouveau_ bohemian, Tiny Blue Trees by anda

Holli Zollinger (holli_zollinger)

The love of the natural world is often evoked in Holli Zollinger's designs (holli_zollinger on Spoonflower), which feature earthy elements and hand-drawn abstracts that feel as timeless as they do current. "Right now I am very inspired by simple design and a natural earthy palette, and I am still deeply invested in botanicals," Holli said. "Geometrics and tribal designs always play an important role, as I love indigenous and global design." Her work evokes texture in such a sophisticated way that you could look at one of her designs online and imagine it has the washed linen handfeel of an heirloom.

One of Holli's strengths as a designer is her consistent use of collections. She groups her designs within the same themes in the Spoonflower Marketplace so they can be combined to complete a look for an entire room or outfit. Color palettes play an important role for her as well, and she's not afraid of jumping between the clean simplicity of soft French blues on off-white and experimenting with color-rich tones, mixing mustard yellow, teals and hot pinks in a combination that is electrifying. Stick within collections of like themes and color stories for your DIY projects, and you can mix and match patterns together like a true interior designer.

For any budding designers out there, Holli recommends staying true to your own style. Whether you're just getting started with uploading your own original artwork or are mastering the art of repeats, she shares words of encouragement: "Let us all feel your special kind of magic!"

Get to know Holli:

What drew you to Spoonflower?

"I found out about Spoonflower in 2008 from a merchant at a farmers' market who was creating her own textiles for product. There was something very enchanting in those first few years as I set out to find my own style and to teach myself how to build a repeat. I feel extremely lucky to have been there from almost the beginning! Spoonflower has been such a consistent and empowering entity in my life, I feel so honored to still be a part of it."

What is your process when creating a new design?

"It most often begins with an inspiration, followed by research of the idea and imagery, and then execution with pencil and pen. After it gets scanned into the computer, the images get cleaned up on Illustrator, and then I begin the process of building a repeat. Lastly, I spend a large amount of time finding the right color palette, which feels incredibly important to the final execution of the design."

What piece of your wardrobe best represents your style?

"Hats! I love that extra little bit of swagger you feel when you put one on!"

Featured holli_zollinger fabrics, from top to bottom: Protea Neutral, Wildflower Seeds Neutral, Mediera Sun Tile Pink, Wildflower Study Dark, Sun Tile Marsala Light; border design Mandala Tile Light

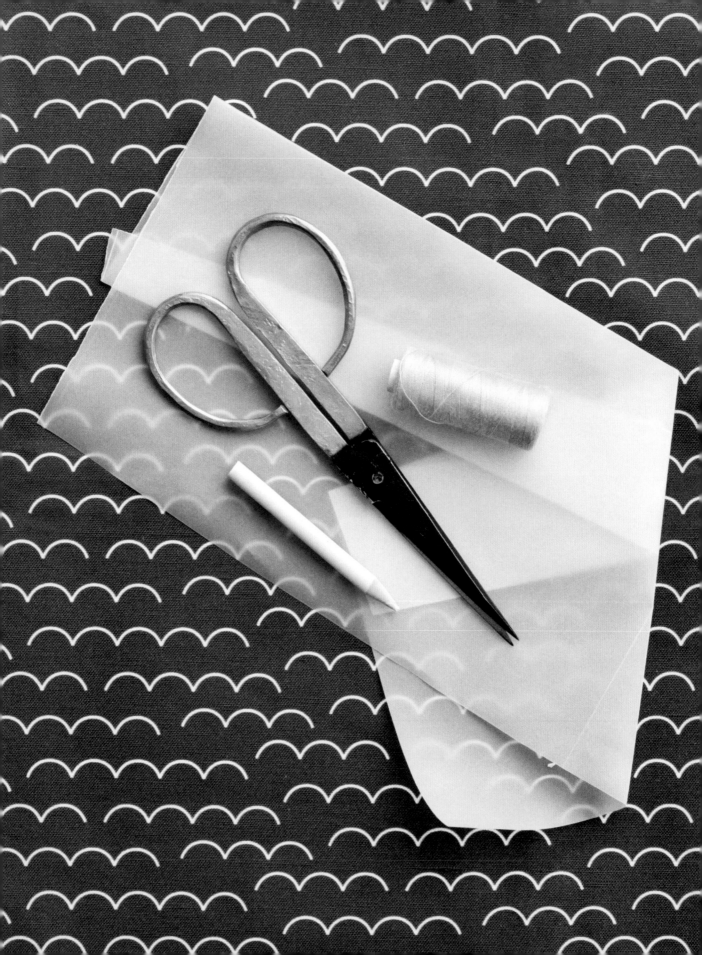

TEMPLATES

How to Use the Templates

Scan the template you need, enlarge manually and then print it on letter (A4) sized paper. When printing, enlarge to the percentage noted on each page— your printer will probably have a box marked "custom scale" where you can type this in. A few of the templates might be larger than the standard paper size in your printer once they've been scaled up, and in this case you'll want to use a print setting that will print the image on multiple pages that fit together when cut out and reassembled. (My printer calls this setting *poster*.) Then, just cut out the two pieces of the template, fit them together like a puzzle, and tape to secure. All the templates include seam allowance as noted in the project text.

Featured fabric:
By the Sea — Waves by lemonni

Dribble Bib

Photocopy template at 135%

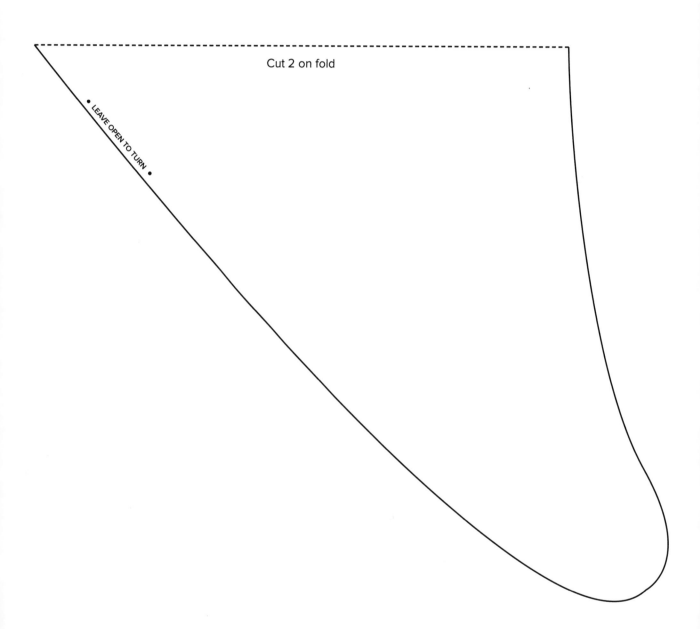

Cut 2 on fold

LEAVE OPEN TO TURN

Pet Collar Bandana

Photocopy template at 135%

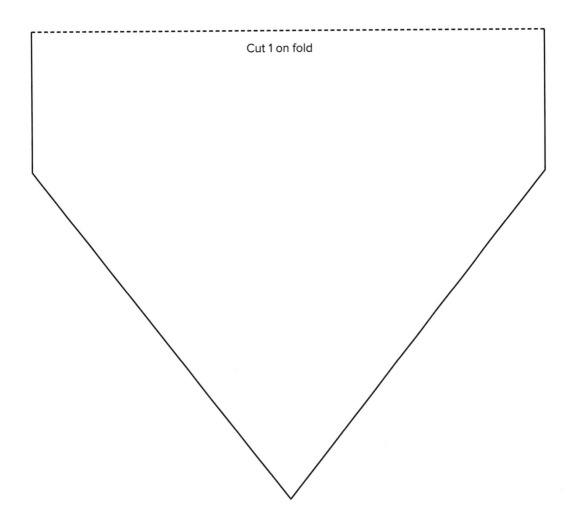

Cut 1 on fold

Espadrilles (size 8/9)

Photocopy template at 125%

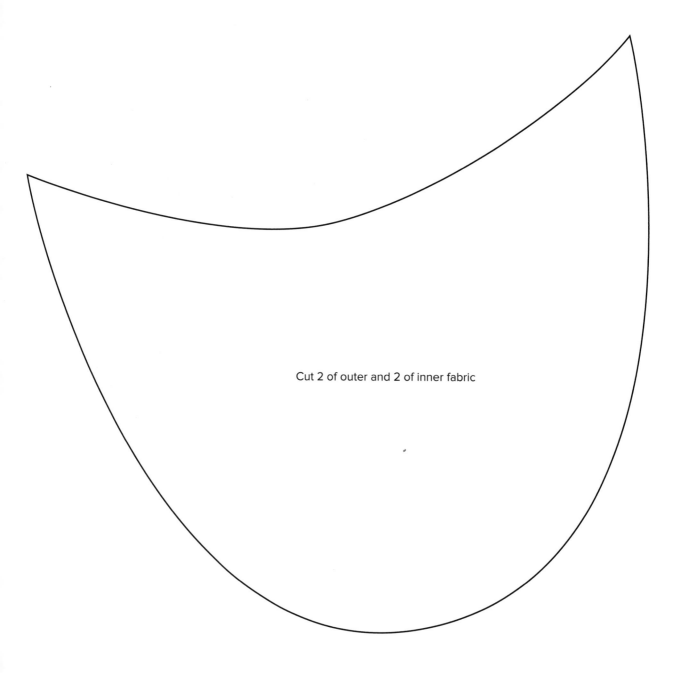

Cut 2 of outer and 2 of inner fabric

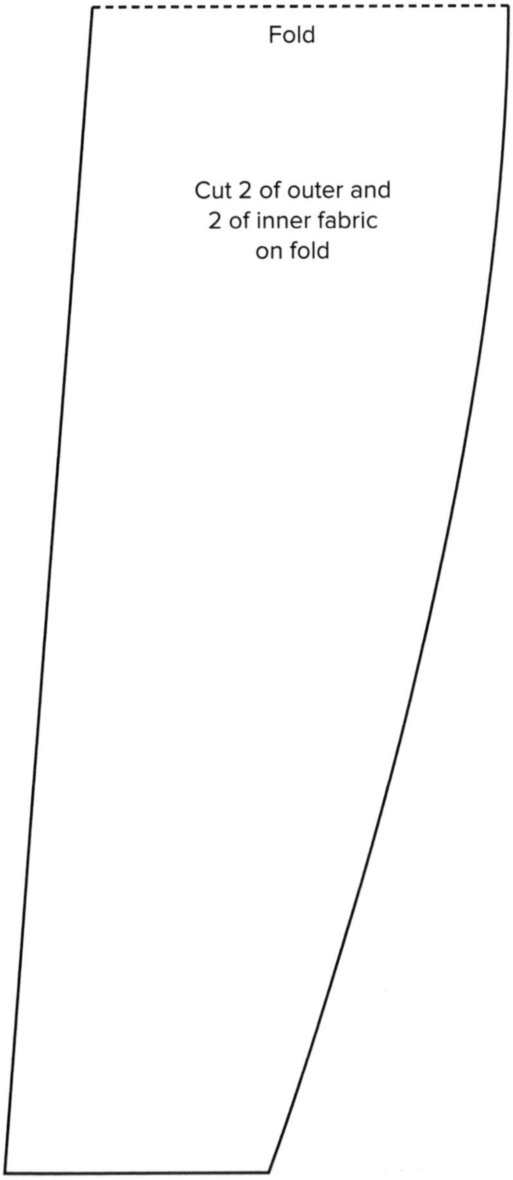

Fold

Cut 2 of outer and
2 of inner fabric
on fold

Tip:

+ When you buy espadrilles
soles, they will often
come with a pattern so
you can make a pair in
any size. I tweaked a
standard ladies' size 9
espadrilles pattern and
have included it here—if
you're a size 9 too, you're
all set! But if you're not,
I suggest cutting the
pattern out of muslin or
scrap fabric then pinning
in place to the sole
around your foot. Then
add or subtract fabric
from the short ends of
the back piece and the
inner curve of the toe
piece in ⅛- or ¼-inch
increments until it fits in
a way you like.

Fleece Mittens

Photocopy template at 125%

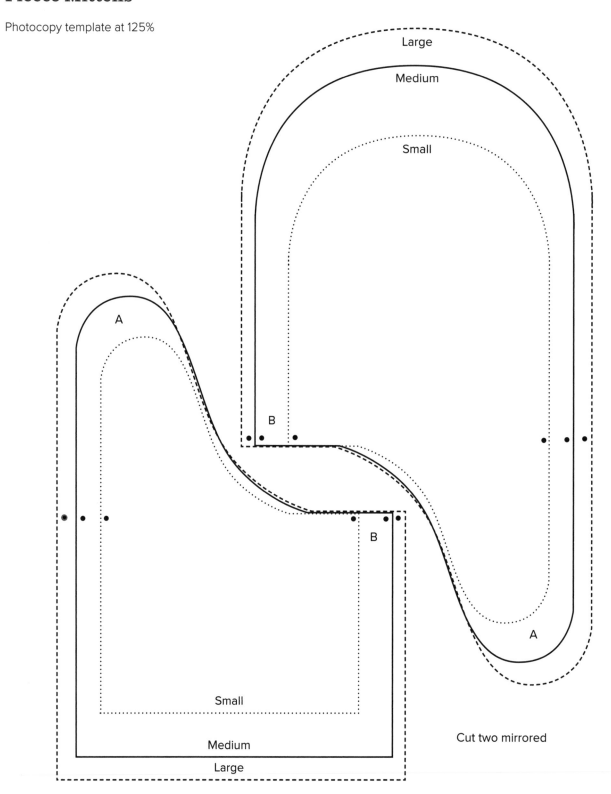

Large

Medium

Small

A

B

B

A

Small

Medium

Large

Cut two mirrored

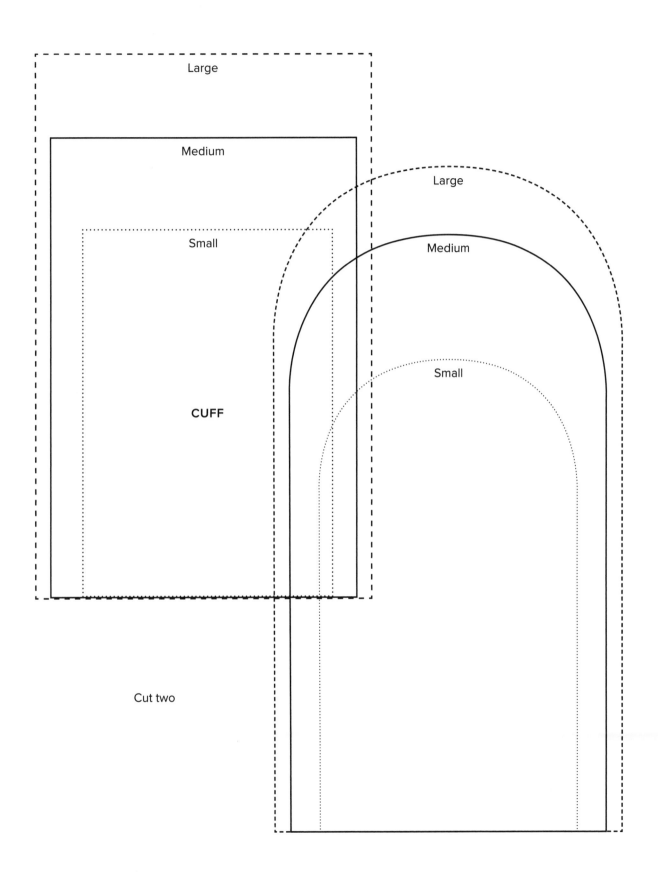

Large

Medium

Small

Large

Medium

Small

CUFF

Cut two

Bike Cap

Photocopy template at 125%

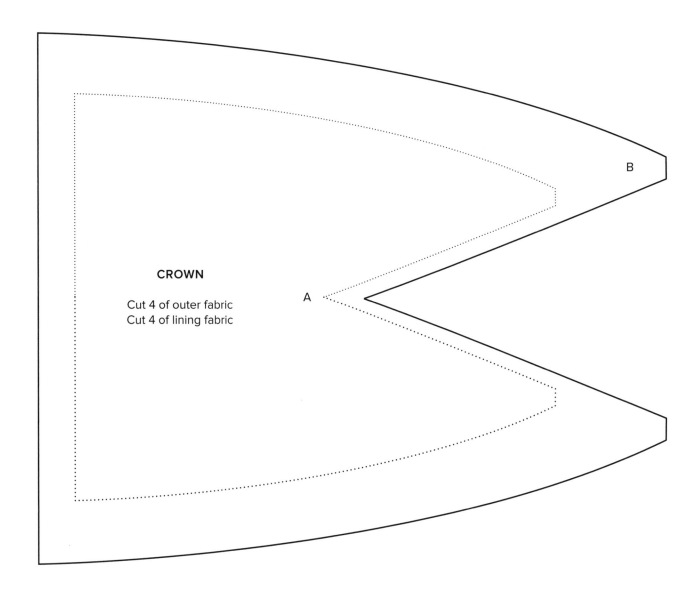

CROWN

Cut 4 of outer fabric
Cut 4 of lining fabric

A

B

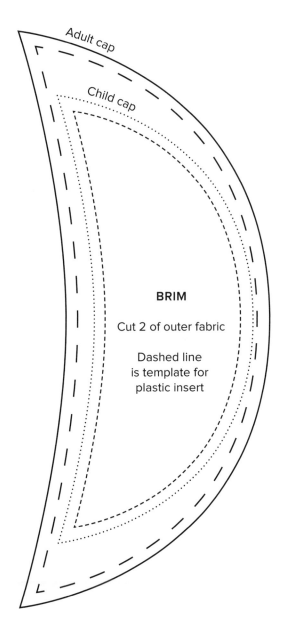

Adult cap

Child cap

BRIM

Cut 2 of outer fabric

Dashed line
is template for
plastic insert

Pop-Up Puppets

Photocopy template at 100%

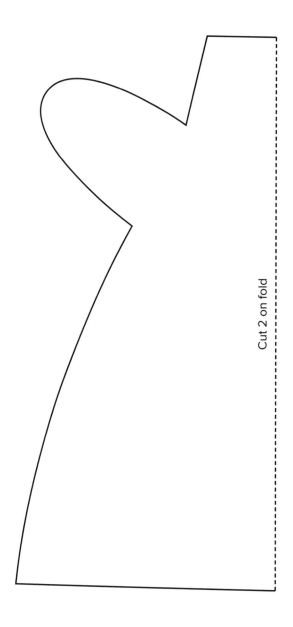

Cut 2 on fold

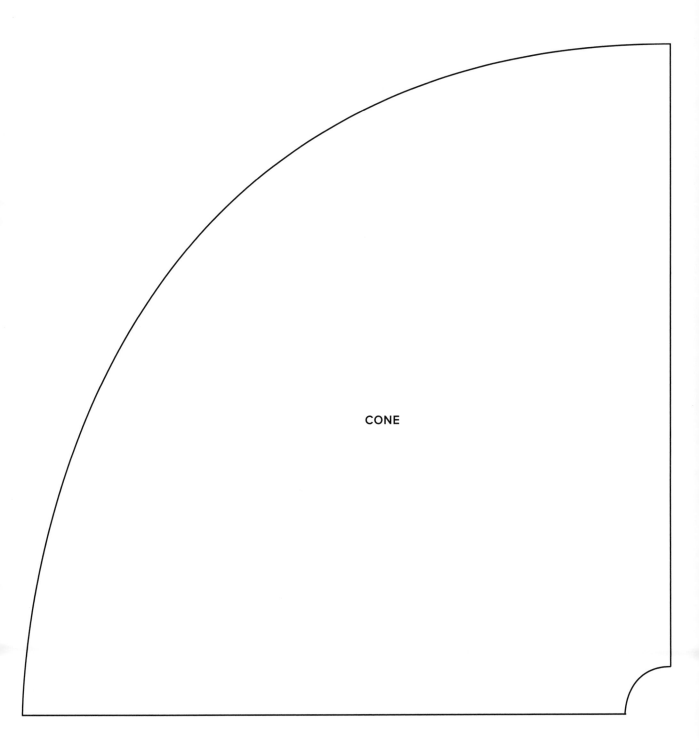

CONE

Advent Calendar

NUMBER TEMPLATE

Scan at 300 dpi and
upload to Spoonflower

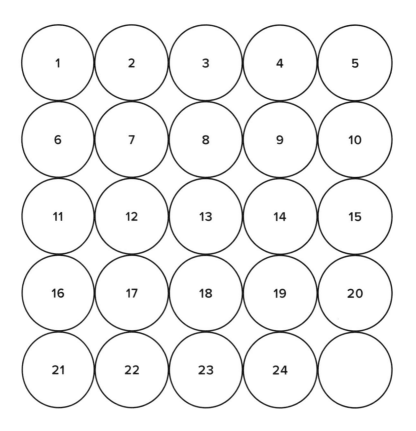

Rabbit Hat

Photocopy template at 135%

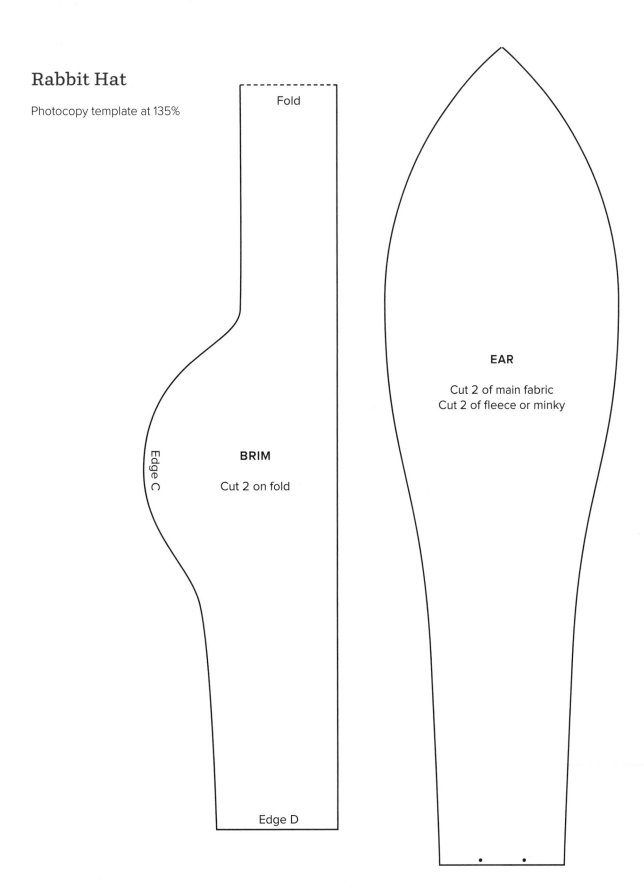

Fold

Edge C

BRIM

Cut 2 on fold

Edge D

EAR

Cut 2 of main fabric
Cut 2 of fleece or minky

Bear Rug

Photocopy template at 135%

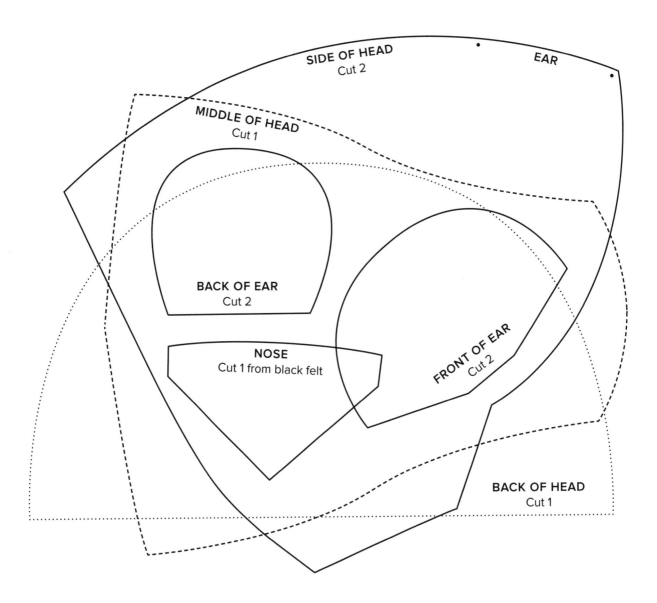

ABOUT
THE DESIGNERS

Have your eye on any designs featured in this book? You can find these and thousands upon thousands more beautiful patterns in the Spoonflower Marketplace from independent designers across the globe. That's what makes us so unique: instead of collaborating with just a few designers, we open the doors to everyone to share a unique aesthetic or vision. In fact, there are over 16,000 designers who sell on Spoonflower (many of whom are earning a living!), and more designs are added every single day.

If you're inspired to start designing on Spoonflower, you can join for free anytime by registering for an account. There are no limits on uploads or revisions, and you always retain full rights to your artwork. If you choose to sell your designs on Spoonflower, you can earn 10% commission on MSRP (on average $2.50/yd sold) with payouts every two weeks, and you'll always earn the maximum, no matter the promotion.

While our commission rates are some of the most competitive in the business, we don't stop there—you can earn up to 5% additional in bonus commissions based on monthly sales volume thresholds. We also post designs to external marketplaces, covering all of the listing and advertising fees, to help amplify the reach of our talented artists. It only takes a few minutes to get started!

Whether you're supporting the artistic community with your Marketplace order or personalizing a project with your own design, the sky truly is the limit.

ABOUT SPOONFLOWER

What is Spoonflower?

Spoonflower is the world's first web-based service for custom, on-demand fabric creation. With Spoonflower, anyone can design, print, and sell their own fabric, wallpaper, and gift wrap. Customers can either design their own fabric or papers or they can shop from Spoonflower's Marketplace of on-trend and niche designs.

From its humble beginnings with just a handful of team members and two fabrics, Spoonflower has expanded to offer over twenty-five different fabrics and three papers. Since 2008, the Spoonflower community has grown to over 3.5 million individuals who use their own designs and the Marketplace to make curtains, quilts, clothes, bags, furniture, dolls, pillows, framed artwork, costumes, banners and much, much more. With over 650,000 designs—and more added every day—the Spoonflower Marketplace is the largest collection of independent designers in the world.

In 2016, with the realization that over a quarter of Spoonflower shoppers were based internationally, the company opened a factory in Berlin to offer more affordable and faster shipping for customers. To welcome even more creative minds to the fold, Spoonflower launched two sister brands for those who relish designs in the Spoonflower Marketplace but want some help on the do-it-yourself aspect. On Sprout Patterns you can design custom apparel and have it made just for you, and with Roostery, you can purchase ready-made home goods and bedding that reflect your personal style.

Spoonflower's Design Challenges

The Spoonflower community consists of over 16,000 designers and 600,000 shoppers. One way we inspire creativity and engage our wonderful community is through weekly design challenges. The spirit of the Design Challenge is to give a creative prompt that inspires designers to introduce a new design to the Marketplace that speaks specifically to the theme we have crafted.

From Botanical Block Prints to Significant Otters, our prompts challenge designers to work in pen and ink, watercolors, digital programs, and more to craft original artwork that entices oohs and aahs. Sometimes we present designers with the added challenge of a limited color palette, and we've even collaborated with companies such as Bucketfeet and Hilton Hotels to give designers a unique platform to gain even more exposure.

The best part is that the finalists are selected by the community—voting is open to all!—and top favorites win weekly prizes for their originality and vision. That means that every week, you'll see fresh new designs in the Marketplace that have been endorsed by an engaged community of shoppers and artists. With a wide range of themes ranging from quirky to elegant, it's the perfect place to discover inspiration for your next project.

Plus, whether you vote in a challenge, add new designs to your favorites collection or order a yard or two, you are encouraging designers to explore their individuality while helping them earn a living at the same time.

How does Spoonflower print for me?

In short, the essence of print-on-demand is the ability to print the exact quantities you want, just the way you want it and with minimal cost to you. Unlike traditional textile printing, which require a complicated and expensive setup, Spoonflower's modern digital printing process gives you the ability to print as little as an 8" x 8" swatch, with no minimums or pricey setup fees involved.

How does it work? It's simple. Spoonflower's large format inkjet printers get instructions from the computer file you upload to the website and can start printing right away—whether you need a fat quarter or hundreds of yards (meters) of fabric or paper. This process allows for a cost effective option not only for individuals who want to make just a few yards of fabric, but also for those printing on a much larger scale, as we offer bulk discounts.

Spoonflower's print-on-demand process is designed to minimize wasted fabric and ink. Fabric that doesn't meet high standards never makes it to the landfill, as it is shredded for industrial applications like car upholstery and furniture stuffing, bedding and flooring. On top of that, the printing process uses water-based pigment inks and dyes that are 100% biodegradable.

It's part of the company's mission to ensure that Spoonflower fabrics are good for you and good for the earth. From the low-waste digital print process and organic fabric options to FSC-certified paper options, Spoonflower seeks to provide products made safely and sustainably.

Featured fabrics: Floral blues by indybloomdesign and Donuts Pink Chocolate by charlottewinter

ACKNOWLEDGMENTS

Anda would like to thank Peter Corrie for literally all things, but especially for still loving me even after I spent one entire summer vacation ignoring our surroundings and children and inventing sewing projects instead. Tim Stobierski for virtually holding my hand and shepherding this text into reality, Suzanne Pozzo for going through it all with a fine-toothed comb, and Shawna Mullen and Meredith Clark for keeping everything together. Tara Reed and Katie Berman for practical advice and fabric suggestions. Allie Tate, Michelle Swart, Maria Neidhold and the rest of the Spoonflower Berlin team for letting me camp out in their office with my Pfaff and make a giant mess. Allison Polish for support and critique, and Stephen Fraser for thinking I might like to tackle this project in the first place. And, the entire Spoonflower community of designers for being a constant source of joy. I'm also eternally grateful to Beau Colin, who styled the photos in this book, for her innate skill with color, texture, and off-color jokes, and to Zoë Noble for her wizardly ability to make any handmade object look amazing. Lastly, thanks and hugs to Sidonie, Alvin, and Alaska for being fantastic young people, natural stars, and hilarious models.

Featured fabrics, from top to bottom:
Tropical Leaves by willowlanetextiles,
Strokes Dots Cross and Spots by
littlesmilemakers, Monstera Leaves
by crystal_walen, Chalk Tribal Stripe
by leanne

Featured fabrics opposite contents page: Palm Leaves King Pineapple by chicca_besso, Woodland (green) by lydia_meiying, Honeycomb Aqua by mia_valdez, Watercolor Floating V's by betsysiber, Geometric Flower Tiles by daniteal, Watercolor Cubes by bluebirdcoop, Kaleidoscope Emerald, Ombre by seabluestudio, Marble Marvel Emerald by lottalorier, Aurora Borealis Black and White by mia_valdez, Hedgehog Squiggles, Small by karismithdesigns, Ink Dot Scales by crumpetsandcrabsticks, Subway Tile Hex by holli_zollinger, Herringbone Tweed by willowlanetextiles, Black and White Laurel by crumpetsandcrabsticks, Tiki Rattan 1d by muhlenkott, Mermaid Gold by crystal_walen, Art, Deco Fans, Gold by magentayellow, Railroad Mini Aspen by willowlanetextiles, Glam Gold Mermaid by crystal_walen, Painted Medallions, Gold by crystal_walen, Medallion Pattern in Mustard by micklyn

Editors: Shawna Mullen and Meredith A. Clark
Designer: Danielle Youngsmith
Production Manager: Denise LaCongo

Library of Congress Control Number: 2017956866

ISBN: 978-1-61769-079-2
eISBN: 978-1-68335-331-7

Abrams books are available at special discounts when purchased in quantity for premiums and promotions as well as fundraising or educational use. Special editions can also be created to specification. For details, contact specialsales@abramsbooks.com or the address below.

ABRAMS The Art of Books
195 Broadway, New York, NY 10007
abramsbooks.com